I0161439

YOU MUST
'C'
YOUR WAY THROUGH

C. RAY CALHOUN

C. Ray Calhoun

Copyright © 2016 C. Ray Calhoun

All rights reserved.

ISBN-13: 978-1539358732
ISBN: 1539358739

Cover designed by Steve Fata

DEDICATION

THIS BOOK IS DEDICATED TO MY LIFE LONG SOULMATE, GIRLFRIEND, AND WIFE, PEGGY ANN (SUE) CALHOUN AKA LADY P WHOSE COMMITMENT TO GOD AND ME HAS BEEN ONE OF THE MOST TREMENDOUS BLESSINGS IN MY LIFE. TO OUR CHURCH FAMILY, FULL OF FAITH CHRISTIAN CENTER AND
IN LOVING MEMORY OF

'LITTLE PEOPLES'

WHO STOLE MY HEART IN A WAY NO ONE COULD IMAGINE.

I THANK GOD FOR THEM ALL.

ACKNOWLEDGMENTS

THANKS TO MY DAD AND MOM, BROTHERS, SISTERS, AND MY IN-LAWS. TO MY WONDERFUL WIFE, PEGGY, THE MOTHER OF OUR CHILDREN, CALVIN II (LIL CAL), COQUINA (SMALLFRYE AKA COCO), T'WANA (NIKI), DEREK (DEREK D.), DONTA (TAY) AND THE FASCINATING LITTLE PEOPLES, OUR GREAT GRAND.

FAMILY IS EVERYTHING!

FOREWORD

Following up C. Ray Calhoun's #1 best-selling book, 'You Can Win in Life' is his sophomore book entitled, 'You Must "C" Your Way Through'. C. Ray is pleased to add an additional chapter to this book and some revisions in some of the chapters. YMCYWT has now become an international best-selling book in Canada, Germany, Japan, Australia, and the Netherlands. C. Ray Calhoun is fully persuaded anyone who feel they can and/or should be doing better, has the potential to do so. Whatsoever you desire or desire to change, whatever you would like to accomplish, what goal you are desiring to reach or achieve, what level of life would you care to possess, and many if not all your dreams can come true when you realize 'You Must See It, Before You See It'. The alpha letter 'C' in this book title is simply a metaphor C. Ray is using for the word 'see' because without faith the change you want, the change you desire and deserve, will not come to fruition. C. Ray has done it again with a book of practicality, simplicity, and productivity when you can believe and seek life's best for you.

H.S.

For I know the plans I have for you," says the LORD. "They are plans for good and not for disaster, to give you a future and a hope.

Jeremiah 29: 11

CONTENTS

You Must
"C"
Your Way Through

By C. Ray Calhoun

1) CHANGE

"You will never change your life until you change something you do daily. The secret of your success is found in your daily routine.   John C. Maxwell

We are God's highest form of creation. No other creation of God has the capability of changing to the degree man can. If we don't like our situation we have the intelligence and will to change it. The first 'C' to see your way through is change must and can happen. It is a common myth that many who succeed in higher levels of life and living possess a gift or talent. That is not true, however, I do believe talents and gifts are certainly advantageous, but not prerequisites to moving beyond the average to levels of increase in areas of life you would desire to ascertain. On your journey of personal growth, you will find your gift and/or your talent. Personally, I barely finish the twelfth grade, ended up becoming drug and alcohol addicted, and had numerous problems with the law. What I'm doing now and what I've accumulated, (by the Grace of God), has nothing to do at all with luck and it defies the belief of so many who knew, (or thought), I would not make it in life.

It all began one day when I had a face to face talk with that guy who cause me all my problems, who led me to become interested in drugs, alcohol, and I eventually became addicted, that same guy who was showing me how to get ahead the quick, easy, and illegal way by stepping on the backs of anyone who gets in the way. One day I went face to face with him, looked him dead straight in the eye and said to him, "Say man, you are the reason I'm in the shape I'm in and you are getting out of my life! You are a screw-up and I'm sick and tired of you! It's time to make a change, and the change starts first with you!" Now after I finish yelling those words out loud, in his face, looking in the mirror with no one in the room but me, I promptly went in the bathroom, washed my face, and begin a self-improving odyssey which has propel me into some of life's best. It all began one eventful day in April at the house of an elderly, un-educated, yet anointed preacher we called Reverend Jacob Taylor, living in the Oak Cliff area of Dallas, Texas.

Most people blame their situation and their life problems on someone else. I recently spoke with a group of people and I listen as one after one blamed their bad predicament on their partner. Your first change should be YOU! YOU are your biggest problem and will be your biggest change. You are where you are and what you are by the choices you've made over the years. When you work at it the change will come, not overnight, but it will and can come if you are willing. There is a 'Law of Process' which simply states nothing of significance happens overnight. If it has taken time for you to get where you are it will take some time for you to get where you want to be. Patience, tenacity, and determination will get you to where you want to be.

You were born to win, but to be a winner, you must plan to win, prepare to win, and expect to win.

In the classic movie, The Wizard of Oz, Dorothy the main character reached a fork in the road and ask the scarecrow, (who was assisting her in locating the Wizard), which one should she take, which direction should she go. After a slight pause the scarecrow ask Dorothy, "Where do you want to go?" She paused, pondered his question and simply said, "I don't know". The scarecrow replied to her, "Then either way will do." The point is you must know or have an idea where you want to go and why. When your WHY is big enough, you will find a HOW, and you will endure any HOW. In my best-selling book, 'You Can Win in Life', I detail what I call "The 'D' Recipe of Success" with life illustrations of how change and development came about by applying the knowledge acquired in life situations. We are not necessarily destroyed for lack of knowledge; we are destroyed for lack of application of the knowledge. Many people know to do right and will not do it. I chat with people daily and they want this, they want that out of life, they would love to drive that kind of automobile, or live in that kind of house, but after all has been said and done with information to lead them to these wants and desires, they failed to do the necessary procedures to get them. In the book, 'You Can Win in Life' the 'D' recipe is a roadmap to a successful life and obtaining any goal, from losing weight, to starting your own business, even to having a better relationship.

This is what was said by one of the many readers and reviewers of my first book:

"There's many recipes for success. For greater success, you need the right ingredients. Follow the five (5) D's and you can achieve it abundantly." - Ronald M. — Book Review ('You Can Win in Life' by C. Ray Calhoun)

Now if you study the wealthy you will realize most of them were and are ordinary people which did extraordinary things. Many didn't realize they had a gift until they decided to come out of their comfort zone. The comfort zone is a bad area and a trap. The comfort zone robs individuals of realizing and recognizing hidden talent, suppressed gifts, and untapped potential. Most of the world and all the average are trapped in their comfort zone. They are afraid and/or nervous to move from it and others think it is okay, while some think they are safe. No disrespect, it is okay for them because they are AVERAGE. We were not placed here to be average, which is acceptable to those that accept it, but average is not what we are supposed to be. I read this in the most amazing book I've ever read and continue to read:

'So here's what I want you to do, God helping you: Take your everyday, ordinary life---your sleeping, eating, going-to-work, and walking-around life--- and place it before God as an offering. Embracing what God does for you is the best thing you can do for HIM. Don't become so well-adjusted to your culture that you fit into it without even thinking. Instead, fix your attention on God. You'll be changed from the inside out. Readily recognize what He wants from you, and quickly respond to it. Unlike the culture around you, always dragging you down to its level of immaturity, God brings the best out of you, develops well-formed maturity in you' – (Romans 12: 1-2 Message Translation).

We are here to raise the standard, to be a light unto the darkness, to be eagles and soar higher than the norm. Fitting in and being average is not what we were created for. We are fearfully, wonderfully, incredibly, sufficiently, and uniquely made. The wealthy are and were people who decided to do what others refuse to do, that others could do, so that they can live like others cannot live.

Many years ago, I felt as if some people are just destined to be wealthy and live a life of abundance which so many others just dream of or don't realize or believe they could achieve. As time progress and I begin to watch life unfold I begin to believe if it's possible for some others it's possible for me. What is the catalyst which propels certain ones into a life of success and wealth? I began to think why can't I be better off? I believe that to be an honest observation of many individuals. Now I say that because there are so many people who desire to be average and don't have any aspirations of a much better life. I'm not one hundred percent sure what all their reasons are but I know that to be many people reasoning because it once upon a time was mine. With all respect, I honor their choice and I believe it is alright for us to choose or not choose whatever life we desire. However, I don't feel that type of individual is reading this book. This book is being read by individuals like yourself who believe in obtaining a much better life, who believe there is more to life than average, who believe that their personal destiny consists of more than barely getting by or even just enough. Some are doing quite well, desire more, and certainly there is nothing even wrong with that. Individuals such as Warren Buffet, Mark Cuban, Bill Gates, and others are still pursuing avenues of increase, not because they are greedy as some say and possibly believe, but because the more they possess the more than can accomplish. These incredible people, countless others are philanthropists, and givers to many worthy causes.

This book also is being read by people who believe, know they were created for so much more, deserve more in life, out of life, and here to be a blessing to more than just me and my three, their four and no more, so to speak. Nothing in one's life will change for the best unless the desire to change becomes evident.

Mandy Hale says, "Change is painful; Growth is painful; But nothing is as painful as staying stuck somewhere you don't belong".

Change is all around and will always happen. People are downsized who thought and believe they would be at the company until they retire. There are those who woke up one morning and the company they work for was gone and/or closed. I worked in the computer field and environment, but I'm not in that profession any longer and haven't been in years. When I woke each morning to go to work never did I envision much more than getting a paycheck and supporting my family, seeing that I married at an early age in life. I never dreamed or thought I would own businesses and be extremely active in a non-profit organization. Change is inevitable, either for good or not so good, that can in most instances be in your control. Accidents and health issues are just a small fragment of reasons which can and do bring about significant changes in one's life. Some changes we can prepare for, however, many significant changes occur unexpectedly and many carry devastating consequences health wise, mentally, and financially.

If you desire to better your relationship, your family, job position, career, your department, your company, your health, and your wealth, you must develop yourself, you must develop in your growth. My good friend and mentor, John Maxwell says, "To develop your wealth, develop your worth". I was in Orlando, Florida with John when I heard him first say that. It was such a revelation to me even though I had heard similar things said but when I heard it put like that I became so excited about developing myself to the next level of what God had for me. Therefore, it's imperative you surround yourself with books, CDs, and information of successful people which will trigger a revelatory button in you and cause you to move in the direction of excellence. Many spend over five hundred hours a year in our automobiles and never realize how this can be turned into a self-developing, faith building mobile university by listening to encouraging and motivating information on cd's. While you are listening the possibility of hearing something which will cause you to tap into your God-given potential and cause an explosion of purpose driven growth plus opportunity!

Eleanor Roosevelt said, "The purpose of life is to live it, to taste experience to the utmost, to reach out eagerly and without fear for newer and richer experience." She went on to say also, "The future belongs to those who believe in the beauty of their dreams."

When you develop, yourself it causes everything around you to become better. God has never wanted us to stay the same. Everything He touched and/or anointed became more, became better, so, in other words he, she, it, and they changed.

The Creator says concerning the subject of us changing and developing, *"I have it all planned out----- plans to take care of you, not abandon you, plans to give you the future you hope for."*

We all need to come to the realization that the plan from the beginning was for us to go from not enough to more than enough. To go from the pit to the palace and not squander our gift of life frivolously. We were created to make our niche in time and the world will be a better place because of our existence. An epitaph of our life should read, "So many others became better off in life because you were here."

The awesome Zig Ziglar, who I had the privilege and honor to meet said, "You can have everything in life you want, if you will just help other people get what they want." Zig went on to say, "You were born to win, but to be a winner, you must plan to win, prepare to win, and expect to win.

One of the first things which engrafted to my spirit when I began my journey of personal growth was an inert desire to help others, to position myself where I could and would be a blessing everywhere I went. There is no true success without the desire to be a blessing in others' lives no matter race, creed, color, nationality, ethnicity, life-style, and/or origin. An ignorance of our society is the behavior toward any individual from another because of the color of their skin which no one had a choice to choose.

George Bernard Shaw said, "Progress is impossible without change, and those who cannot change their minds cannot change anything."

Know this that the thinking which has you where you are in life now must be changed for you to move to the next level of life. For as a man or woman thinks, so are they. Change your thinking and your life must change! You must acquire knowledge and to do that you must read the right information, you must listen daily to the right information, and you must begin to associate with people who are going somewhere in life, not just out to eat, party, and have a (supposedly) good time. It's okay to enjoy life and I'm a strong believer in that area, however, life is enjoyed to the fullest when finances are no longer an issue and we are adding value to others lives. I believe it was Mark Twain who said, "The person who does not read has no more advantage over the person who cannot read."

Change is inevitable, growth is optional.

Growth is optional is not speaking of your age or size, it's speaking of your personal development to enhance your own insight, perception, and ideology. If you don't grow yourself on a regular plan, then you will become the average. Again, average is not evil or even bad, but average people usually don't read books like this. And if they, the 'average', decide to pick up and read a book like this it's because they desire not to be average any longer and something inwardly is pulling them to a higher level. When you develop your mindset to the next level then your actions began to line up with your new thinking and your renewed mind will cause behavior which is conducive to better choices leading to a much better life. This is a realization which if comprehended at an early age will cause us to begin sooner than later to soar to higher heights of prosperity and accomplishments. When we don't take control of our life changes in life will.

A greater future belongs to those who are daring enough to risk being uncomfortable moving out of their comfort zone, challenging life head-on with a different perspective, and planning. Most people if you ask them what their plan of growth is they will begin to inform you of how they are going to do this, how they are going to do that, they are going to have this, and after all the rhetoric they share in the end looking deep into what they have said will ultimately bring light to the fact they have no plan. In several of the Master Mind Group sessions I facilitated one of the assignments were for each participant to ask ten people what their plan of growth was. All the responses we received, not one, was a definitive plan of growth. Here's the sad part, all of them which responded thought what they said was a growth plan and it wasn't. Some knew it wasn't but failed to admit they didn't have one except one or two did respond with the answer of not having a growth plan. That's not so bad, here is my point, if you don't have one, get one. If you don't know how to get one, ask somebody. There are so many proud and arrogant people of financial lack which are committed to staying that way because of pride. People who are living beneath their means and living check to check and perpetrating this lifestyle which has them one to three paychecks, if missed, away from losing it all. I know, I've been there, and it was scary all while I was there. Many people are living beneath their means and refuse to acknowledge the fact that they need help. One of the main reasons is the fact that they want to take the position that everything is all right. What is the meaning of 'everything is alright'? That was something I used to say and for a long time I thought it was alright until I started realizing as far as I was concerned everything being alright was a non-effectual, non-producing terminology, which kept me average. Remember this, change, growth, success, and potential have no ending destination, they are ongoing and continual. Many finish school and/or college and live as though that was the end of their personal growth.

Eleanor Roosevelt said, "Great minds discuss ideas; average minds discuss events; small minds discuss people.

John Maxwell in his book, The 15 Invaluable Laws of Growth, says this about change. "When you want something you have never had, you have to do something you have never done." He goes on to say, change is always possible, so remember these truths about change. Change is personal and to change your life, YOU need to change. Change is possible, and everyone can change. Change is profitable, and you will be rewarded when you change.

2) COURAGE

Definition of fear: Fear is a feeling induced by perceived danger or threat that occurs in certain types of organisms, which causes a change in metabolic and organ functions and ultimately a change in behavior, such as feeling, hiding, or freezing from perceived traumatic events. Fear in human beings may occur in response to a specific stimulus occurring in the present, or in anticipation or expectation of a future threat perceived as a risk to body or life; Extreme case of fear can be a freeze response or paralysis.

I was fearful of staying the same, working until I was sixty-five or seventy, retiring on an income less than what I earned working full time, knowing while I was working, it was never enough then. Now I'm thinking once I retire, and they keep moving retirement age up, will I be needing to return to work or get a job at seventy-five just to make ends meet. Also, there is that lingering thought based on information you hear that social security income, as we know it today, may not exist in the very near future.

"Everything you've ever wanted or desired is right there on the other side of fear."

It takes courage to grow up, become who you are, and who you are meant to be. If someone would have told me I would be Senior Pastor of a growing ministry, owning businesses, helping others to start, their own businesses, acquire certification from the prestigious John Maxwell Team to coach, speak, train, and teach, certified in domestic violence, abuse counseling to work with law enforcement departments in different cities, writing # 1 best-selling books, and helping others to write their stories I would have never in a million years believed it. It is a portion of my destiny; it is who I was meant to be, what I was meant to do up to now. The other side of fear allowed all of that to come to fruition and there is more to come. There are robbers in your life and you must recognize one of their names is fear.

Over the year's fear of the unknown has robbed countless people of their God-given destiny. As outgoing as I am many avenues of something new was, as with most, a daring and frightful adventure. I can remember some things I would not attempt because I was afraid I couldn't do them, or I perceived I wasn't capable of doing them because of lack of intellect or out of my comfort zone. In the definition of fear words to notice are, perceived, anticipation, freeze response, and paralysis. Many won't start a business or any campaign because of perceived failure. The thought it may not work. They negatively think themselves out of an incredible future that they will never experience because of fear and/or self-doubt. They anticipate negative outcomes concerning their endeavors. People have a 'freeze response' when they think of coming out of their comfort zone to do something different.

There are one million reasons why a person shouldn't do this, shouldn't start that, don't give this a try, don't attempt this, but there is one reason why you should, which supersedes the multi-million reasons, (I call excuses), that you shouldn't. It is what I refer to and call 'the Winning Factor'. That winning factor that transcend any excuse, that transcend any reason to not move into your destiny, that transcend anything you've been told why you couldn't and why it won't work, that singular winning factor which no one has but you, is YOU! Too many anticipate failure before they even get started and thusly their response is to freeze up and not do anything. I once read the best way to get started on any endeavor is to get started. If you don't know how to start or even what to start, ask somebody. There are life coaches, trainers, and individuals such as myself who can help and assist you to find what you are good in or what may be a good fit for you to begin. There is no reason you cannot move into the next level of life-style you desire or even have dreamed of.

"Courage is the most important of all the virtues because without courage you can't practice any other virtue consistently; Courage is not the absence of fear, it's the going on in spite of fear."

I was fearful of changing careers because I didn't know anything about garage doors. I was a white shirt, black tie wearing technician working in the computer programming environment. My friend mention earning more money, but it wasn't anything like what I was doing. All kind of thoughts were circulating inside my head. Maybe I better remain where I'm comfortable and know what I'm doing. However, when he mentions to me the earning potential of what he was doing it caught my interest.

It is amazing that if the WHY is big enough the HOW becomes less important as being an excuse for not achieving.

I worked in the computer industry on what was called the second shift from 3 pm to 11 pm, which allowed me to ride with him during the morning and sometimes part of the day to learn what he was doing. You must understand when you want something bad enough you must be willing to do whatever is necessary to move into your next level of destiny. I eventually learned enough and was hired by the company who employed my best friend. I begin to earn more income and I was about to come face to face with my next level of growth.

Dr. Robert Anthony says, "Courage is simply the willingness to be afraid and act anyway".

Within a relative short time, I became interested in starting my very first business. I found myself driving down the road about to talk myself out of it. I was thinking, I don't know how to run a business, I don't know anybody who started their own business. I started remembering the people who told me guys like me who claim they would be doing their own business just sit at home most of the time and didn't do anything more than watch TV. They told me it wasn't going to work because who was I to even think about having his own business. I was thinking I don't have any clients, no customers, most of all, no money, no start-up capital, and wasn't for sure about how to go about even getting a business started. When I mention it to my wife I thought she was going to call those people that bring those white jackets out that ties in the back. Who was I, the, barely made it out of high school graduate, to even think something so ridiculous? I decided if it wasn't going to work I would find out first hand. I knew if I didn't even attempt it, it wasn't going to work. So, I decided to give it my best shot.

Ralph Waldo Emerson said, "What lies behind you and what lies ahead of you, pales in comparison to what lies within you".

Now some thirty-one years later, not only is that

business still thriving, but I've initiated several other businesses and endeavors. You are and have been created to be the winning factor in any area of life you desire if, and only if, you believe. As we mature we become a product of our environment. The way we think, and our behavior has developed from the people we have spent time with, the places we've been or haven't been, the school(s) we've attended, and the books we've read, or in most cases the books we failed to have read carries an enormous weight on us concerning how we think, our behavior, and our potential. It has a direct correlation to the things we have courage for or the things we are fearful about. Our self-esteem is directly affected by our upbringing.

One of the areas of my life which I had low self-esteem was when I found myself in the presence of college educated individuals. I would not speak much so they wouldn't realize how ignorant I might seem to be. I come to a broad realization which is, and I say this with respect, no matter what level of education one possesses, he or she is no better than me and me no better than he or she. I've found out in life in many areas the A and B students of college and higher learning end up working for the C and D students with high school education and dropouts. Your level of courage will only heighten as your level of faith heightens. I can remember speaking for a major auto dealership in Dallas, Texas thinking within myself as I stood in front of this group of well-dressed educated professionals wearing suits and ties listening to me. After I finish my speaking engagement they all lined up for an autograph copy of my best-selling book. One guy purchased four of the books for each member of his family.

It is imperative you develop your faith and faith comes

by hearing repeatedly. Then you must first believe in a greater force than you and second is faith in yourself. Fear will always raise its ugly demeanor, but faith will always carry you past it and through it.

When fear knocks, faith opens the door, and nothing is there.

I been told the term 'fear not' is in the Bible 365 times and I believe that is one important encouragement for each day of the year. Embedded in you are so many gifts, talents, which the world needs, and will be better with if you just don't hold back. Give your God-given destiny a chance, become all The Creator has purpose you to become, and perform all HE has sent you to accomplish.

Mark Twain said, "Courage is resistance to fear, mastery of fear, not absence of fear"

I can remember as my first company begin to grow and develop I place a contractual bid for installation of several very large commercial overhead doors with the City of Cedar Hill right outside of Dallas, Texas. When I first went and evaluated the project I was overwhelmed at the size of the doors which would be needed. I pondered this situation and I remember thinking to myself I haven't did anything on this magnitude of service since I started my company. I was thinking about the additional part-time workers I would need to hire and how long would it take to do something of this magnitude.

There again I found myself about to talk myself out of it. We are incredible beings and can solve any problem we are facing. We have been designed by The Almighty to accomplish whatever we put our mind to, however, just as our minds carry the ability to solve problems it also carries the ability to create excuses, especially in the presence of fear. After contemplating this project, I decided to place a bid with the City of Cedar Hill to perform the installations. After a week or two I thought some other company bid was better and I was somewhat relieved I didn't get the job. I decided I would call and inquire. The lady who answered the phone place me on hold and after a few minutes came back on the line and informed me one company had my company's beat. I politely told her thank you and hung the phone up.

Approximately three or four weeks later this lady call me back and informed me the company which had given a better bid could not do the project as they had bid, we were the next in line for the opportunity, and would we be available to perform the work necessary to complete the job. I had mixed emotions of happiness, because it was a very nice contract, and fearfulness because it was an enormous job, the largest at that time of being in business. I even went back down to the job site and stood inside the building looking at the huge doors which would need to be installed. Ladders, lifts, extra personnel, and safety were just a few of the important tasks I was considering.

After going home, a good night sleep, and prayer I accepted the bid and proceeded to initiate steps needed to begin and complete the job. After four weeks, five additional employees, and many hours the job was completed, and I patted myself on the back. We all high five one another and all the guys were saying when they first arrived at the job site, day one, they were wondering if I could do it and how were we going to accomplish such a project. One of the guys who had work with me before on much smaller jobs said to the other guys he knew I would figure out a way to get it done.

There are people who believe in you sometimes more than you believe in yourself. In life, you will find some who say they believe in you but are waiting for you to fail. I've found out in life to be all that God wants you to be and do all God has purpose you to do, we need both kinds of people. It is because of them both many times we have an internal surge of energy from The Creator which causes us to prove to them and ourselves we can do it.

James Allen said, "People are anxious to improve their circumstances but are unwilling to improve themselves. They therefore remain bound."

One of the reasons I decided to come out of my comfort zone and do something for myself is because I didn't like the results I seen with other people who did what I was doing. Working until they retire and attempt to live on a portion of income which while they were working and getting full pay was just getting by. I know people who work on a job for years that they do not like. I would hear people say things like I been working here for a long time but if I find something better I will leave, yet they aren't seeking anything better because they are comfortable in their surroundings.

Conformity is the enemy to progress.

Do not be conform to this superficial world and be sucked into the 'state of average', in the city of 'barely getting by', on a street named 'I'm doing okay.' Use your Google Maps and you will find most people living right there! Your best life will come outside of your comfort zone because it causes you to face fear and being uncomfortable to reach the rewards and growth you are destining to achieve. Whenever you decide to come out of your comfort zone there will be self-doubt and low self-esteem issues. In the book of Judges, a young man named Gideon was hiding and threshing wheat because his nation was being oppressed by a neighboring nation which took all his nation's goods. When Gideon was called to rescue his nation from their enemies and told God was with him, he begins complaining and stating that if God was with him why was all these bad things happening. God reminded him that his nation disobeyed, even started worshipping foreign and false gods. Then Gideon informed God his clan was the weakest in the nation and he was the weakest in the family. Here we find an example of low self-esteem and finger pointing.

All of us, if we are honest and true to ourselves, will usually attempt to find an excuse for not coming out of our comfort zone.

John Calvin Maxwell says, "Achieving a dream is about more than just what you accomplish. It's about who you become in the process."

No one wants to be uncomfortable, however, once we recognize life's best will only come from us stepping out and going forth to better and greater things, then we will utilize the power within to do what we already know is necessary for change.

Calvin Ray Calhoun says, "The Power to Win, Comes from Within."

The Bible consistently speaks to those in the book and us to 'be of good courage'. As I mentioned earlier, it is widely known throughout the term 'fear not' is found in the King James Version three hundred and sixty-five times which is awesome knowing our calendar year has the exact amount of days. It is common and natural that fear will raise its ugly presence, excuses usually follows, and these are some of our greatest thieves of destiny. The most effective way to rid yourself of fear tendencies is to feed your faith.

George Mueller said, "If we desire our faith to be strengthen, we should not shrink from opportunities where our faith may be tried, and therefore, through trial, be strengthen.

Faith is the connection to your fulfilling of your God-given destiny. Fear is here to rob you of your faith to be all that The Creator has destined you to be. Faith is the bridge which leads you from where you are to where you would like to be.

Famed actor Harrison Ford performed in a series of movies where he portrayed, a fictional character by the name of Dr. Indiana Jones, a college professor of archaeology. "Indiana" Jones's full name is Dr. Henry Walton Jones Jr., and his nickname is often shortened to "Indy". In the movie, Indiana Jones and the Last Crusade, the third installment of the Indiana Jones movie series filmed in 1989, Dr. Jones's father played by Sean Connery (Henry Sr.), receives a mortal gunshot wound in his abdomen from the character Donovan to force Dr. Jones (Harrison Ford) to retrieve the Holy Grail with its healing power if he wanted his father to live. To retrieve the Grail, he would need to undergo three "literal" tests of courage and faith. After overcoming two of three traps he finds himself deep within the cave, standing on the edge of a cliff needing desperately to get to the other side separated by a huge bottomless pit opening. As he pondered how to get to the other side being too wide to leap he begin to remember what his Dad murmured to him about having faith. He closed his eyes lifted his leg up slowly and leaned forward. As his leg came down it stopped as though in midair, Dr. Jones somewhat bewildered looked down, then reached down, picked up some sand, tossed it in front of him, and to his surprise the sand revealed a bridge which was unable to be seen because it was hidden and disguised by means of camouflage.

You already have success in your future, but it is hidden and sometimes camouflage by fears of failure, insecurities, and doubt. You must be willing to lift your leg and step out on faith. You must develop your faith, learn to live by faith, and not by sight or emotions. Your faith is your bridge to the other side of life fulfillments, better relationships, and increase.

I speak to numerous youth groups throughout and recently I informed this youth group, which I was honored to speak to, a lesson in life. As time goes on you will decrease in friends but the quality of your friends will increase. Some friends you don't need because of the negative influence and possibly other unfavorable traits. Many friends are there to see what they can get from you and once you stop allowing them to be in on your blessings they will become your enemy. Some friends are temporary anyway. They are there only for a season. Learn to love people but put your full trust in God. We live in a time where people despise your success, but act like they don't. People search and look for a reason to be offended and usually find one. I teach not only the youth but also the not-so-youthful, to learn to understand life and people. Life is not always fair, and people are not always nice.

Realize how people are, how they act, and rise above it.

Be the one they envy because of your kindness and love.

Many leave you because they can't match you! Be the one they can't stand because of your success, your favor, and your blessings. True and real friends understand your weaknesses and admire your strengths. Friendship means understanding, not always agreement. It means forgiveness, not forgetting.

"Fake friends are like shadows, always near you at your brightest moments, but nowhere to be seen at your darkest hours."

Those 'friends' that leave when you are down were never with you at all from the beginning. They were with your success, not your character. Through life notice the ones that leave and if you don't mind missing them then it was good they left. Don't try to prove anything to anyone but yourself and be yourself. When you try to be someone else they aren't there, and you are not there either because you weren't being yourself by trying to emulate someone else. Always remember The Creator already know you better than you know yourself and you should know yourself better than anyone else. People see you from the outside, but true friends know you from the inside. Learn to smile when they don't, laugh when they're mad, and soar while they crawl.

Augustine said, "Faith is to believe what we do not see, and the reward of this faith is to see what we believe."

You must understand courage is essential. Fear will rise every opportunity it can. We have been commanded to be of good courage. Moses had led the people for many years, he had died, and the responsibility fell on Joshua. Thrown into an enormous role of leadership I'm positive he was approached by fear. There is a command from The Creator which says, "Have I not commanded you? Be strong and courageous. Do not be afraid; do not be discouraged, for the LORD your GOD will be with you wherever you go." (Joshua 1:9) Translated from the Message it says, "Don't get off track, either left or right, so as to make sure you get to where you are going............Haven't I commanded you? Strength! Courage! Don't be timid; don't get discouraged. God, your God, is with you every step of the way."

Courage requires faith and where faith is courage will be also.

One of the greatest attributes of courage and strength is to forgive and the world thinks it's a sign of weakness. A weak person rarely forgives because forgiveness is an attribute of the strong. A brave person acknowledges the strength of others. You are stronger than you think. When you are weak, our strength comes from relying on HIM! Time and time again it is mention in the scriptures to 'be of good courage'. It tends to render the thought if we need to be told many times then many times we are faced with the reason why we need to be told.

3) COMMITMENT

Abraham Lincoln said, "Commitment is what transforms a promise into a reality."

Mr. Francis and Ruth Calhoun have been married for sixty-eight years on November 6, 2016 and still married, they are my parents. Charles and Mary Calhoun have been married for 43 years and still married, they are my brother and sister in law. Lee and Kathleen (Calhoun) Delley have been married 45 years, they are my sister and brother in law. Francis Jr and Sharon Calhoun were married 12 years and she passed on a Monday morning at work. He stayed unmarried for a while and raised his two girls, then met Pat, they married, have been married 13 years now and still married, they are my brother and sister in law. Peggy, my high school sweetheart, and I have been married 43 years, still married, and still my 'girlfriend'. I met Peggy in January of 1971, she was in the ninth grade and I was in the eleventh grade. Two years later I knew I had a GOOD one and I married her while she was in the eleventh grade. She was seventeen and I was eighteen, turning nineteen fifty-five days later.

One of the most important and major factors in success or failure, be it marriage or divorce, winning or losing, above and not beneath, ahead or the tail, average or above average, wealth or poverty, life of abundance or life of just getting by, owning your own business and the success of that business or closing the business, the important factor that causes it all to stick together, work together, and come together is COMMITMENT!

Put God in charge of your work,
then what you've planned will take place.
(Proverbs 16:3 – Message Translation)

Commitment is the glue that bonds your goals. Commitment is doing the thing you said you were going to do long after the mood you said it in has left you! Most people fail to accomplish, not because of lack of desire, but lack of commitment. There are only two options regarding commitment: you're either in or you're out. There's no such thing as life in between! The question I ask many of the clients I coach, "Where are you with this commitment? Are you in or out, because there is no in between." When a person has solely committed to achieving, they choose the mental capacity to focus on problem solving because there will be obstacles which will get in your way. Therefore, it is of utmost urgency one becomes committed to his or her program no matter what it is.

Mario Andretti said, "Desire is the key to motivation, but its determination and commitment to an unrelenting pursuit of your goal – a commitment to excellence – that will enable you to attain the success you seek."

The world has given a false meaning to commitment because there is so much lack of commitment in our world and society today. No one finishes anything anymore hardly and no one sticks it out for the long haul any longer. Too many relationships are all about convenience, not commitment. As soon as it's not convenient anymore or as soon as someone feels tired of another, they depart and go their separate ways.

On New Year's Day millions of people make New Year resolutions. They go to the gym, they start eating healthy, and they turn a new leaf on life over. One to two weeks later, the gym is no longer packed by all those who came the first week of the year. The new healthy diet has been replaced by old eating habits which was stopped for a week. That new leaf on life which was turned over has been flipped back over and that same old behavior is back. The commitment level of the majority has no meaning at all. When an individual has set his hooks into commitment nothing can hold him back.

When I begin my first business, the garage door service, I had no clients, no starting capital for a business, but I was committed. I sold the family car, our only car, for just enough money to buy a truck. An old brown Ford pickup truck with no heater, no air condition, and no radio. You could see the street through a hole in the floor of the truck and it had a standard shift transmission, not automatic. The rubber on the tires were so thin you could see the air. I called my truck tires 'May Pop' because those suckers (tires) may pop any second now. For the next year or so the tires did just that many, many times and because of my lack of finances my wife was somewhat furious to say the least that I had sold family car for that truck. I begin seeking jobs, to build my garage door service, by putting out hand written flyers, knocking on doors, and making phone calls.

Emerson said, "What you do speaks so loud I can't hear what you say."

Daily my wife would ask did I earn any money and it was very annoying and frustrating because many days I hadn't. She would on a regular basis tell me to get a 'real job' because what I was doing wasn't working. Now you must understand we had five children, (I assisted my wife in raising six, the five children and me), and making ends meet was extremely difficult. Many months the ends never met. The money, what little that came in, ran out before the month ran out. It needs to be understood, my wife was just wanting a better life as so many people do even today. I would inform her that my father worked for a company for twenty-two years and they locked the doors and close the company overnight. I was determined not to be in that position in life to have that done to me or anything like that. I didn't want someone with the ability to end my livelihood any given day without me having any say so or not being aware of it.

I was committed to building my own business. True commitment is like a pit bull dog you latch on and don't let go. In the Bible, a guy by the name of Jacob had an opportunity to grab hold of an angel. Once he caught hold of the angel he would not let go. He held on and wrestled with the Angel until the break of day. The angel said, "Let me go, for the day has broken." But Jacob said, "I will not let you go unless you bless me." And the angel said to him, "What is your name?" And he said, "Jacob." Then the angel said, "Your name shall no longer be called Jacob, but Israel, for you have striven with God and men, and have prevailed." Jacob was committed to getting out of life what he wanted by any means necessary. Commitment is holding on, not quitting, continuing until you get what you were going after.

In the Bible names carry significance. The name Jacob meant trickster and much of his life was about doing just that, with his brother, his father, and anyone he encountered, until that eventful day, but after that, his name was changed to Israel which meant 'he wrestled with an angel of God' and committed to not letting go until he received what he wanted.

Martina Navratilova said, "The difference between involvement and commitment is like ham and eggs. The chicken is involved; the pig is committed."

I continued building my business because something deep down inside of me kept saying you can do this. I had informed my wife when I purchased that old brown truck that something inside of me kept saying if you get you a truck, the truck will get you another car. Well sure enough the truck did get us another car, another truck, and a better life. We now have several trucks and several cars. When I purchased my wife her first Mercedes Benz S-class I ask her if she still wanted me to go get a real job. None of our friends or family members owned a Mercedes Benz at that time. Success eludes so many because they don't know the meaning of commitment. All of us can think of a time when we didn't stay to our commitment and didn't finish what we started. When we grow and develop ourselves by daily commitments of a personal growth plan we will reach levels of success and accomplishments because it is commitment which will propel us into some of our best days and ultimately to a better life.

Those who have succeeded in life, especially financially, have many things in common and one of the important task the successful have is a commitment to hard work. They work hard early, so they can work light later. Commitment is a fear reducer, commitment is a motivator, and commitment is the connector to you achieving your God-given destiny.

We all should desire to reach levels of finances where our monies work for us.

Thomas Edison attempted, some say, over seven

hundred ways to introduce the world to the concept of light. It is reported his assistant encourage Mr. Edison to give up and quit. Thomas Edison said to the young assistant with a smiling face, "Oh no young man, we now know seven hundred things which does not work". I would say Mr. Edison was committed.

Commitment causes you to have a deaf ear to your naysayers and negative, toxic people. The ones who say you can't do it and hope you don't because in their mind you would be better than them. (And they would be right) Not better as a human being but better because you decided to be above average for a more abundant life which has been promised to you and they decided to be average. Every promise comes with a condition which, when obeyed, will place you in position to receive what the promise is. There is no automatic promise from God where mankind should do totally nothing. Believers say 'salvation' is free, but it has a condition which must be met to receive even it. One must believe in their heart and confess with their mouth. The point is, so many want everything free and/or easy. The best things in life are not free and easy. Anything that has worth and worth having is worth going after.

Get a mentality of commitment and watch you reach levels of achievement you had only dream of. Commit to working consistently toward your goals, your vision, and your dreams. It is through committed consistency and diligent work, coupled with tenacity, patience, and flexibility, that you will ascend the ladder of success. There are no 'get rich quick' programs. I know of people who listen to some who have seemingly done well financially and the individual leaves the prospect thinking it's going to happen overnight or in a month or two. They many times failed to share the real, honest fact in becoming financially secure, and failed to inform others concerning the process which is better served with patience, focus, and endurance. I've heard it said it's lonely at the top and it is if you are there alone. So, my goal is to take those, who are willing and ready to sacrifice a little now for a whole lot later, to the top with me. It is plenty room at the top because most are not there.

President Barack Obama said, "Making your mark on the world is hard. If it were easy, everybody would do it. But it's not. It takes patience, it takes commitment, and it comes with plenty of failure along the way. The real test is not whether you avoid this failure, because you won't. It's whether you let it harden or shame you into inaction, or whether you learn from it; whether you choose to persevere."

Find your 'why' and become committed to it and the rest, as they say, will be history. The 'why' is what has made many wealthy and is the catalyst to begin your journey, your process, of you becoming the person necessary to acquiesce your 'why'. Your 'why' will affect everything and everything changes! Your 'why' brings clarity to your purpose and helps you to see clearly the reason. You 'why' causes you passion, inspire you to be all you are purposed to be and accomplish. Your 'why' will make a difference in your personal life, in your family's lives, your friends, your company, your business, and your career. Your 'why' gives a visible difference in your walk and your talk. This is the time commitment is crucial because much will come against you in your pursuit of your 'why'. One of the biggest reasons most people do not find their 'why' nor accomplish it is non-commitment.

While competing in the marathon in Mexico City, John Stephen Akhwari due to the high altitude of that city, began to cramp up in his leg. Akhwari was not quite adapt for the high altitude in his training and at the nineteen-kilometer point during the forty-two kilometers, there was jockeying for position amongst several of the runners and he was knocked to the pavement where his shoulder encountered the pavement, received a bad wound on his knee and causing a joint to dislocate. He however continued running, finishing last among the fifty-seven competitors who completed the race (75 had started). The winner of the marathon, Mamo Wolde of Ethiopia, finished in two hours, twenty minutes, and twenty-six seconds. Akhwari finished in three hours, twenty-five minutes, and twenty-seven seconds to a small remnant of a crowd which was left at the stadium sitting under a sunset evening. A television crew was sent out from the medal ceremony when word was received that there was one more runner about to finish. As he finally crossed the finish line a cheer came from the small crowd. When interviewed later and asked 'WHY' he endured such excruciating pain, amidst others with less reasons which quit, and continued, Akhwari said, "My country did not send me five thousand miles with a commitment to compete in the marathon and just start the race, they sent me five thousand miles to finish the race. NOW THAT'S COMMITMENT TO A 'WHY'!

Why is there little to none of anything written about the eighteen which quit during the marathon? There is never much written about quitters because anyone can do that, and many do. So much the world could have and so much could have been accomplish if so many had not quit on their dreams, their goals, and their purposes. A person which has commitment in their heart does not think about quitting and quitting is not an option. You must go down swinging, fighting before you quit and give up. This is the mindset of the committed. If a person has no 'why', has no goals, desires, and/or dreams of succeeding a person's level of commitment will never reach its maximum potential.

One must find a cause, a 'why', and reach a level of commitment, be loyal to that commitment, because there will be trials and tests you may have to endure which will be demanding. There have been several times in my development early on the white flag of surrender was nearly waived, but I remembered my 'why' and I continued.

Sometimes life will slap you in the face and it will feel like you were hit with a wet rag. It will sting and hurt leaving you wondering why so much pain. I quit saying and thinking to myself, 'why me'. That small inner voice starts reminding me each time something unpleasant happened to me and I thought 'why me' it was indicative of me wanting it to happen to someone else. That was not what I wanted or was thinking for something to be unpleasant or hurtful for anyone else, so I decided to quit saying it and thinking it. It was another step in my progression which propel me to the next level of personal success and growth. If you are a person which says or think that, like I was once upon a time, I encourage you to not justify saying or thinking that, but to pause and calmly think about what you just read. That small inner voice said to me, "if not you then who?" That was enough for me because I know when something is brought to my awareness which I need to consider, meditate, and then proceed. Too many people have not listen or ignored that small inner voice we all have and now they don't fail to recognize it anymore. Many of their decisions, especially those which end in disaster, could have been avoided had they not lost the ability to hear, recognize, and obey that small inner voice. Some call it intuition but whatever it's called by the different people it is there to help and guide us.

Dr. Martin Luther King Jr said, "If a man hasn't discovered something that he will die for, he isn't fit to live."

4) CHALLENGES

'Strength doesn't come from what you can do; It comes from overcoming the things you once thought you couldn't.'

It is your God-given destiny to go from a land of not enough, through the land of just enough, (This is where you will find the average and most people), on your way to your land of more than enough. On your way to your land of more than enough you will encounter challenges. There will always be giants in our way. Giants of discomfort, giants of fear, giants of setbacks, giants of opposition, giants of past failures, and giants we haven't met yet but will be in our path as we travel to our destination. David had a giant in his way to a better and more fulfilling life. Moses and the children of Israel had giants in their way to their land of more than enough. I had my giants along the way of growing my business and developing myself to become what THE CREATOR had purpose me to become.

God's best for you will lead you on a path where you will face challenges and giants in the land. Challenges causes us to face our fears and convictions of inadequacies. Challenges causes us to face our low self-esteem issues and when we deal with our challenges through faith and actions the result will benefit us and move us to the next level on our stairway to success. You must come face to face of the realization your biggest challenge will come from within. Our potential lay dormant until we tap into it and begin to develop into our full potential.

An old African proverb says, "If there is no enemy within, the enemy outside can do us no harm."

The biggest challenges we experience do not come from our life situations or outward conditions, our greatest challenge is conquering ourselves. We many times are a product of our environment. This means our thoughts and our behaviors have been developed by what we have seen, what we have heard, what we have experienced, and the people we have associated with as we became older. The Apostle Paul said, "Woe unto me this flesh (self) I'm in. When I want to do right, I do wrong." If this incredible individual had problems with himself, then we certainly have problems with ourselves.

The flesh is lazy if it's allowed to be. The flesh of man and/or woman is directly opposed to you achieving success of any kind and it will fight you every step of the way. It takes a greater force inside of you to cause you to be a winner consistently against your adversary. Your flesh is warring against your spirit's creativity, initiative, drive, and will win in many instances. It is up to you to fight it, to know first you are in a battle, and the winner is you, not your flesh. The Apostle Paul said, "I discipline my body like an athlete, training it to do what it should." How many mornings did I experience not wanting to get up and go out, but I did? How many times did I want to splurge (spend money) on something frivolous because I had experience a good monetary week knowing there were higher priorities of necessity, but I didn't? Your spirit understands 'delayed gratification' which means to delay gratifying your flesh when you are aware this is the time to build and when you practice this principal of delayed gratification your reward will be so much better. When the business begins to bring in a profit I can't count the times I faced challenges of going with the guys, buying a suit or pair of shoes, numerous other activities which was not part of the plan, and certainly would have stifle achieving the next goal I had set or even stopped me from reaching it. You must develop 'yourself'.

> **I recently heard Joel Osteen say, "Fifty percent of people who finish high school never read a complete book the rest of their life."**

Reading is the number one best method to improve yourself. Reading increases your mindset and develops your imagination. Reading will develop your mind to ideas you never thought of before. Reading will cause you to speak different and act differently. Modern technology gives us the advantage of listening to audio reading, and listening to someone read a book is okay, and that's better than nothing, but when you read it is something more beneficial one receives inwardly which does not come by listening to someone reading the book for you. When you read, it increases your pronunciation and enunciation. There is and has been an old, somewhat true saying, if you want to keep important information from people put it in a book. I read years ago that eighty three percent of people who start reading a book never finish it. I have a modest library in each of my three offices and I confess I am part of the eighty-three percent with some of the books. I have quite a few books I have read completely and some I have read over again completely, however, many of the books I have started reading I have not finished yet. Usually along my times of reading I will finish those completely also. The key is read something of substance, meaning value being added to your personal development, your ideology, and not just entertaining. Some say the sum-total of who we are come from the books we've read, (or not read), and the people we've associated with regularly. Show me your five closest friends and I can predict your future almost perfectly. Birds of a feather do flock together. If you don't have five closest friends I wonder is it, you that could be the problem? There is no true success among yourself. We make a living by what we get, we make a life by what we give.

Queen Esther could look out for her own personal health or take a chance and be killed for looking out for others. She chose the latter, entered the king's court, and if the scepter was raised all would be well but if the scepter was not raised she could be beheaded. After a moment of silence, the king slowly raised his scepter. You can never go wrong doing something from your heart for others but always remember to be wise as a serpent but humble as a dove. Don't be misused and abuse continually. God has never wanted that for any of His people.

It has been said giving of one's time is one of the most valuable things you can do because time can never be retrieved. Since your time is so priceless then you need to evaluate who is getting it and who you are spending it with. We are to be adding value to people everywhere we go, and our very countenance should light up a room when we enter. It is imperative you pick and choose who you spend your time with. Some people are time stealers and time wasters be careful and prioritize your day. There are people at different places of business I frequent that tell me when I walk in they are hoping I get in their line. There is deep down inside of you a light placed there by The Creator and the more you develop yourself the brighter that light becomes. When you improve, yourself you improve how well you handle challenges. Developing your worth will always develop your wealth. Improving yourself through a planned growth program is the best investment you can and will ever make. When you develop, yourself you will reach what I call 'water rolls off a duck's back' level. This level is for those who when face with challenges handle them with ease and poise. Those things, incidents, issues, and challenges that are out of your control you allow it to roll off your back like 'water rolls off a duck's back'. Challenges are there to improve us when we handle them accordingly. Challenges will make you better or bitter and 'I' makes the difference. The only difference between those two words is the letter 'I' which means you are the difference between those two words when faced with a challenge. A challenge will help us to discover gifts, talents, and power buried in us we once never knew we possess. We grow and develop into what God desires of us more so during challenges than doing the good times. When everything is going in our favor that's all good and well, but our potential is better initiated with challenges than good times.

Mark Twain said, "The person who does not read has no advantage over the person who cannot read."

I have found over the years the people which handle challenges best are the people who have developed themselves best. Challenges come in all forms and the key to overcoming the setbacks in life is the belief that 'this too shall pass'. You must keep in your heart this is creating in me what is needed to produce a winner. You must keep in your heart a truth that all things work together for the good. Most often it takes years of failures and setbacks to become an 'overnight success'. Let's take old honest Abe, Abraham Lincoln, at a critical time in his life endured the death of his sweetheart, had two failed businesses, and even a nervous breakdown. It is reported Mr. Lincoln attempted to be elected to a public office approximately ten or more times and was defeated in each election. It was later because of his endurance, commitment, and conquering challenges he later was elected President of the United States. During your success journey, there will be seasons of purpose and preparation. Moses preparation for his purpose took forty years in Pharaoh's palace, forty years on the backside of the desert, and forty years with children of Israel.

In the story of Moses and the children of Israel, by promise, had been given a life of abundance in a place called Canaan. A land flowing with milk, honey, and oversized fruits. Twelve spies were sent to observe the land before the multitude would enter. I believe this was done to give the people a vision of entering and to heighten their faith. However, their spirits were dampened because the land was what was told to be but there were giants in the land and instead of faith being strengthen, doubt was strengthen, and their fear heighten. All but two of the twelve were frighten and decided it wasn't worth fighting for. In life, the best things are worth fighting for. The two, Joshua and Caleb, were told in their spirit, 'You Must 'C' Your Way Through'. They saw what the other ten could not see. Jesus is The Master in seeing what others cannot see and enabling us to do the same.

William Shakespeare said, "Our doubts are traitors, and make us lose the good we oft might win, by fearing to attempt."

In life people get a glimpse of what a better and more prosperous life could be on TV. Also, in their own life, maybe even from their own neighborhood, witnessed someone go to the abundant life and for a brief, fleeting moment changed their perspective on living a dream come true type of life.

Some spend just a moment thinking maybe that could happen to me. With all due respect, 'No' it's not going to happen to you, 'YOU' must happen to 'IT'! People who go from their neighborhood to acting in Hollywood, professional singing and/or celebrity status usually have a story of their journey. Steve Harvey, Les Brown, and even myself have this in common, we were all homeless for a moment of time in our journey. When you believe enough to start your journey you will face a challenge or two, you will see a giant or two, and along the way something will cause fear to raise its ugly face and you must not allow doubt to rob you of God's greater blessings. Doubt is one of life's greatest robbers of destiny and it has robbed so many with gifts and talents to settle for an average life.

Challenges in themselves are not always bad because challenges can fuel your faith or fuel your doubt the pump is in your hand. When I'm at the gas station I have the pump in my hand and I can choose to fuel one of my automobiles with regular fuel or super unleaded, but it's my choice. When challenges arise, and they will, you have the choice to fuel your faith or fuel your doubt. Out of the twelve spies, two fuel their faith and ten fuel their doubt. Ten of the spies did not enter the destiny God had for them, the land of greater blessings, because of doubt, unbelief, and fear. Two entered in because of faith in the promise given by The Creator, but most of all, faith in themselves.

At first, they will ask why you're doing it. Later they'll ask how you did it.

Wilma Rudolph, born on June 23, 1940, in St. Bethlehem, Tennessee, was a sickly child who had to wear a brace on her left leg. She overcame her disabilities to compete in the 1956 Summer Olympic Games, and in 1960, she became the first American woman to win three gold medals in track and field at a single Olympics. Wilma had every reason not to do much of anything because she had a disability but decided she would not be limited by her shortcoming. Can you imagine what was said to her after her brace was removed and she said, "I'm going to run in the Olympics?" I know she had some naysayers and some even laugh but she blocks out all the negativity and went on to become not just a conqueror but an overcoming conqueror. You must realize the greatness in you is just waiting on you to remove your 'brace', your self-perceived limitations and trust yourself to prove others wrong and become what The Creator has purpose you to become.

If it doesn't challenge you, it doesn't change you.

Many should probably not read this story I'm about to share. I'm an alumnus of the John Maxwell Team and in March of 2016 while attending one of our semi-annual meetings in Orlando, Florida, I had the honor and privilege to meet a guy by the name of Nick Vujicic. Some of you reading this might recognize that name. Nick started an organization called 'Life without Limbs' which derived its name from Nick himself. Born with no arms and no legs he has overcome challenges the extreme clear majority of us can't grasp. We think we have challenges and that's not to minimize serious incidents in all our lives but to be born without arms and legs is what I consider catastrophic. Nick is an Australian born with a rare disorder characterized by the absence of legs and arms. Nick has two small and deformed feet, one of which he calls his "chicken drumstick" because of its shape. Originally, he was born with the toes of that foot fused. Consequently, an operation was performed to separate the toes which would enable Nick to use them like fingers to grab, turn a page, or perform other functions. Now he could use his foot to operate an electric wheelchair, a computer, and a mobile phone. Nick does note and say without reservation he had an "amazingly normal childhood". He was bullied in school and ridiculed. After his mother showed him a newspaper article about a man dealing with a severe disability when he was seventeen, he started to give talks at his prayer group. Nick started his speaking engagements at 19. His very first speaking engagement was at a school over a hundred miles away and he finally talked his brother into driving him there. Nick accepted the engagement before realizing how far away it was. He was paid fifty dollars which he gave to his brother who drove him there. Nick now speaks all over the world has thousands of opportunities and each year he must turned down engagements for the inability to be at all of them. My question is, "What's your excuse?"

In 2007, Nick founded Attitude is Altitude, a secular motivational speaking company. Nick also starred in the short film The Butterfly Circus. At the 2010 Method Fest, Independent Film Festival, he was awarded Best Actor in a Short Film for his starring performance as Will. On his webpages, in a self-formulated "Statement of Faith" Nick states his adherence to born-again Christianity, to classically Calvinist notions on sin and redemption and to Biblical inerrancy without specifying what understanding of Biblical inerrancy he intends to mean. His tenets of faith also include the imminent Second Coming of Christ. He does not publicly identify with or adhere to any denomination or congregation. Nick is married to Kane Miyahara and the couple have two sons and live in Southern California. Nick shared with us just to maintain his necessities each year is approximately two million dollars annually and he is not struggling in the least.

Now after that we just have one choice and that choice is to make it happen.

The first challenge I can ever remember arose when I acquired the disease polio in my early childhood. Polio is a serious disease that affects the nerves of the spine and often makes a person permanently unable to move muscles. Polio is a contagious viral illness that in its most severe form causes paralysis, difficulty breathing, and sometimes death. The doctors had given a not so good prognosis to my parents that the likelihood of me ever walking again would be slim to none. Of course, in this day and time, the cure for polio has long been found and the likelihood of our youth acquiring it now is slim. The cure was found in 1954, the year I was born. Approximately 2 years later I became infected and my mother was wondering that day why I wasn't walking like all the days before. My lower body was paralyzed. After taking me to the doctor I was diagnosed with the disease and fitted with lower body braces which at that time was bulky and weighty. Though the memory is vague in some spots I can remember dreading to see that 'woman in white' coming because she would cause me so much pain. I was too young to realize or know that the woman was a therapist and the pain was from her giving me therapy to help me walk again if possible. Now the world will know where this saying came from, "NO PAIN, NO GAIN", originally came from Lil Ray Ray in the projects of west Dallas.

Approximately three years later around my fifth birthday the braces had been removed and Ray Ray has walked, run, swimmer on my high school swimming team, played basketball at my high school, and the rest is history. I do have a small case of scoliosis which has one of my legs a centimeter or two shorter than the other, but had I not shared that most would never know. Life is full of challenges and challenges can be full of life. Look at your next challenge as an opportunity to perform. Challenges are life changing and you must allow yours to change you for the very best.

Joseph faced challenges from his brothers who wanted him dead because of jealousy and threw him in a pit. His next challenge was being sold into slavery not supposing to be even available to be sold. If that wasn't enough his next challenge came in the house of the Chief of Security and falsely accused by the Chief's wife of improprieties and thrown in jail. Each challenge brought Joseph closer to his God-given destiny by the choices of attitude, integrity, and personal development to make the best of every opportunity. Ultimately, he found himself where God wanted him and where he belongs, second in command of the most powerful nation on earth at that time. Where is, God taking you each challenge you are facing? He will allow you to reach your God-given destiny when you realize the challenge is part of the process and way you are headed. When you face, a challenge remembers............THE BEST IS YET TO COME.

One of our greatest strengths against stress is our ability to change our thoughts.

5) CONTROL

One's greatest challenge is to control oneself.

During counseling, I would many times find the need to inform the counselees, when and if you don't take control of your life, life will take control of you. So often life takes control of individuals through their relationships mostly with family, love ones, and friends. Too many marriages have fallen apart because couples allow others to control how they treat one another, how they operate their household, and in many cases, how they raise their children. In-laws have been the outlaws of relationships. Respectfully, some people have wonderful in-laws, however, that is not the norm. People can tell you how to run your household and what you should tell your spouse after their fourth relationship ended. When you live each day to please someone or help someone more than you should then they have taken control of your life. It is time for you to take control back. You have help them repeatedly, even giving them financial assistance continually because they always have an issue or excuse why they can't meet their financial responsibilities. You have baled them out of situations several times, many times causing you, your spouse, and your family to needlessly struggle. And even if it's not such a struggle to do this it remains a crutch for them and lost control for you. I've told countless number of people to learn the 'magic' word, "NO". It is absolutely amazing The Creator is all knowing and perfect in HIS wisdom says;

2 Timothy 3: 1-5 / Don't be naïve. There are difficult times ahead. As the end approaches, people are

going to be self-absorbed, money-hungry, self-promoting, stuck-up, profane, contemptuous of parents, crude, coarse, dog-eat-dog, unbending, slanderers, impulsively wild, savage, cynical, treacherous, ruthless, bloated windbags, addicted to lust, and allergic to GOD. They'll make a show of religion, but behind the scenes they're animals. Stay clear of these people. (The Message Translation)

I have helped people along the way, I have given to people to be a blessing, and I have assisted people I believe very much and, in the end, when they can no longer get from me what they want my name went from 'sucker' to 'mud'. People will forget the one thousand things you do to help them and remember the one thing you didn't do they wanted you to. If others are in control of you they are happy and many times you are not, especially when you start sensing you are being taken advantage of and your kindness is now being taken as a weakness. I have heard some of the very best excuses for me to continue to give to them and the excuses are fresh and new each time they feel the need to return. They have attempted to make me feel guilty because of their bad choices and horrible mismanagement of their funds, as if it's my fault for what they used their money for. I have learned people will pay for what they want and begged for what they need, then attempt to make you feel guilty for not getting them out of the hole they've dug.

Maya Angelou said, "You may not control all the events that happen to you, but you can decide not to be reduced by them."

My wife and I find ourselves helping people on a regular basis. We believe we have been blessed by God's grace to be a blessing. Lack and not having sufficiency certainly has numerous problems but we've become very aware having an abundance brings about another set of problems and issues also. Saying that, I've personally realized, the problems associated with the lack of finances overwhelmingly outweighs the issues which are brought about by having sufficiency. I've also realized the Bible has much to say about lack, famine, and slothfulness. Many times, these go hand in hand for the recipe of insufficiency.

"Don't be too fond of sleep; you'll end up in the poorhouse.
Wake up and get up; then there'll be food on the table."
(Proverbs 20:13 – Message Translation)

The road to success does not include doing little or doing nothing. The average does those and the above average reach deep down inside finding the necessary inner drive to propel them when others won't. That is what I call a 'go-getter.' The control-stealers will take advantage of the good at heart. You will never get control back if you continue making decisions emotionally. I understand the desire to help everyone because of love and affection. Change not and your situations change not!

Albert Einstein said, "The height of insanity is to keep doing the same thing the same way and expect something different."

Janet Jackson, the sister of famed, pop star, & also known as the King of Pop, Michael Jackson, had a song some years ago called Control. Here are some of the lyrics:

This is a story about control;

My control of what I say

My control of what I do

And this time I'm going to do it my way

I hope you enjoy this as much as I do

Are we ready?

I am cause' it's all about control

And I've got lots of it

When I was 17 I did what people told me

Did what my father said,

And let my mother mold me

But that was a long time ago

I'm in Control – Never gonna stop

Control – To get what I want

Control – I like to have a lot

Control – Now I'm all grown up

My point is she became aware of how important 'control' is. If you are to win the battle of control you will need to become 'all grown up'. As I often say, people grow older, but they never grow up. When you take control of your life you will begin to feel better, things will be better, and you will notice a joy that has been missing for a long time. Taking control is not an overnight occurrence and it will be uncomfortable. Be prepared to take little steps one event at a time. It took years for you to get good at giving your control away now allow some time to develop your self-control. Your biggest control issues will come in the arena of your finances, then family, and you are to use these beginning steps to start your road to reinventing yourself.

One of the issues which comes with financial abundance is the mentality many carry which says because you have it and I don't you should help me. I've even been told, "If I had it I would do such and such with it." First, no one knows what they would do or not do until they are walking in the shoes of the person they are speaking of. When you allow people to manipulate you to do what they say you should or what they think you ought to do you have given them control over you. People have asked for loans and I have given them the loan to help them along the way. First, I ask why they need it, what caused them to be needing it, and I ask what day are they choosing to return the loan? I have learned over the years I am in control of my money and if you request to borrow it I have the right to ask any question I deemed necessary. To avoid me asking you questions is a very simple formula, just don't ask for a loan. People are humble, kind, and nice when they ask for the loan, however, sometimes returning the loan brings about a different behavior. Many times, they don't return it on the day they said. When they do return it, their countenance is like the whole world is on their shoulder. Their attitude many times is as if that day is the worst day of their life. If they don't return it on the day they chose and it's late the best excuse I've heard in a long time is usually given. Everyone knows I am a 'no excuse' guy and it's also how I coach my clients. There have been times when people promise to pay the loan back and never do. When they see you it's as if they never borrowed it. If they don't mention it, then I don't either. What I'm smiling about inside is that I never should concern myself with that individual ever asking again. The good part is I am not affected financially at all. Another person added to the 'don't loan' list. The Bible recommends not loaning and being a surety (co-signing) for a loan. It goes on to say if you do then you are to cover it if they fail on it and you have no right to address them concerning it. Once you have performed the surety you have given your control of that situation to that person. The Bible say we should share and give but it doesn't support becoming surety for anyone. Some of the few who chose not to pay the loan back would, after a length of time had passed, attempt to returned and ask for a loan again hoping I didn't remember they didn't pay the loan back last time. I politely informed them they had been added to my 'don't loan' list. See control can be subtle and the 'control stealers' are very good at their game. You will need to 'up' you game or the control stealers will continue to control you through their unsuspecting ways. I have given money to many people and did not require them to return it because I had a 'leading' to do just that but be careful some of those will return again and again if you allow them control over you.

Nicholas Bon Hoffman said, "A person of character lives by set, certain, and immovable standards."

I am a family person and I believe highly in the bond of family. My grands and great-grands think I'm the second-best thing next to The Almighty. There was one great grand sixteen-month-old, Ka'Niya aka 'Little Peoples', who had complete and total control of me and I wouldn't have it any other way. With all due respect, some of the greatest control stealers come in the guise of family. Parents, children, grandchildren, relatives, in-laws, and spouses can take control of your life knowingly, unknowingly and un-purposefully. Please understand there comes some control you rightfully lose when children and family are involved but it can easily become unhealthy control when it stifles behavior and growth. When it causes you to be unbalanced, mood swings, to be negative, cynical, and you are starting to cease from achieving your dreams and goals, it is unhealthy. Sons and daughters allow parents to control them well after they have graduated college and parents allow children to control them especially 'only' children. I've met and even known several 'only' children, those which have no siblings, and in the clear majority are usually somewhat spoiled rotten and selfish. I've met grown men who still are connected to their mother as if they are still infants. They live in their mother's house and wouldn't have a place to stay if it wasn't for their mother. I'm not speaking of those which live with a parent for health reasons or age concerns but are not willing to take on the responsibility of owning their own place.

Here's another note of importance. He or she who angers you has control over you.

I have witnessed time and time again how people will purposely do things to anger others and in retaliation the people have made choices which caused them hardships, long term trouble, and even confinement. I've seen families torn apart because of choices made during a fit of anger. When a person is out of control the results are usually not healthy or wise. People tend to allow others to offend them. Here's a truth about being offended. No one can offend you unless you allow them to. Offended people offend others. I took my offence emotion and threw it away. No one can offend me unless I give them permission. Learn to give others the benefit of the doubt, whether you should not, give it to them and one day the benefit of the doubt will be given to you.

You can do one thousand good things for someone and they will only remember the one thing you wouldn't do for them.

Each Sunday the National Football League entertains us by allowing teams to meet and play a game to see who has the best team for that day. They go up and down the football field to reach the goal line and score. It is imperative they have a goal to reach and they will never score if they don't reach their goal. Many people are not having the success in life which The Creator has set forth for them because they don't have a goal. You can never score unless you reach your goal. Goals give you something to reach for and gives you focus. Goals are set to propel you to an achievement, better life, and greater future. Goals allow you to control the direction of change in your favor. There is little to no achievement without goals. Most people don't have goals or never set goals and I believe much of it is because many have failed short of their goals and ambitions from high school.

The tragedy of life is not reaching your goals; the tragedy is not having a goal to reach. Setting a goal is important but it's more important what you become while reaching it.

If you think back it was someone or something that took control of your life which ultimately factored into being a part of the failure. Recently I learned there are four components of flying and they are lift, thrust, drag, and weight. If you are to fly high and take control of your God-given destiny you must realize the four types of people in your life. Have you ever thrown a Frisbee or seen one thrown? It flies because of these four forces. These same four forces help an airplane fly. The four forces as I mentioned earlier are lift, thrust, drag, and weight. As a Frisbee flies, lift holds it up. The Frisbee was given thrust when someone threw it from their hand into the air. Drag from the air made the Frisbee slow down and its weight brings the Frisbee back to Earth again. Airplanes utilize the exact same proponents during air travels. Thrust is a force that moves an aircraft in the direction of the motion. It is created with a propeller, jet engine, or rocket. Air is pulled in and then pushed out in an opposite direction just as a fan does. Then lift is the force that holds an airplane in the air and most the lift is created by the wings of the airplane or aircraft. Drag is the force that acts opposite to the direction of motion and tends to slow an object. Drag is caused by friction and differences in air pressure. When you hold your hand outside of a car window while it is moving, and feeling it pulled back, is a good example of drag. Weight is the force caused by gravity which is indicative of things up can and will come down.

Now that I've given you my expertise on piloting let's move this into people and you taking control. When you take control or begin to take control of your life four types of people will be there. It's up to you who you allow in and spend your time with. There will be people who 'lift' you up and encourage you to be all you can be. They will spend positive time with you and have you feeling better when they leave you than when they arrived. They are the ones you will grow to love being around and look forward to seeing them. They will always have something good to say and yet be very real with you in a positive way. Then you have those which will 'thrust' you into ideas, visions, and dreams simply because it is the reason they were sent your way. These people will wonder why you hadn't thought of something great already. They will always be throwing ideas around to generate positive feedback and potential start of something great. If you mention an idea, your dream, or starting a business they are the ones who says, "Great idea, why haven't you considered doing that or starting that?" When they leave, you will spend much of the evening thinking about why you hadn't performed what's necessary to get it done. They leave you smiling and thinking about what if I give it my best shot. The lifters and thrusters are what we need. Then there will be people who 'drag' you down to their level. When they come, and you mention what you're thinking about doing they will tell you how it probably won't work and their cripple, bifocal wearing, uncle or someone they know tried that and failed. Well those people aren't you. They will have nothing good to say and will search for something negative to say. They were born not to be wild but to be negative! They are so negative if you get them in a dark room they will develop! I'm talking negative.

Just think about it right now and you know some and we all do. Just the fact you're reading this book tells me that's not you. Then you have those which will 'weight' you down. I'm a positive, uplifting type of guy, and some people when they come around I feel like I've been holding five hundred pounds up over my head when we part from one another. These people have so much gossip and bad things have happened in the last week they couldn't wait to dump it on someone. If they gossip to you, they will gossip about you. These people are what God writes about in Hebrews, "Set aside every WEIGHT that so easily beset you". You had a smile but now that smile is upside down and you go away from that person feeling like you been under attack. I have said to myself, "I lost thirty minutes which I can't get back."

Carl Sandburg said, "Time is the most valuable coin in your life. You and you alone will determine how that coin will be spent. Be careful that you do not let other people spend it for you."

If you are to take control and begin a new life of winning you must understand it will not be easy. Once again, anything and everything worth acquiring or having is worth giving your best for it. Everything is vying for your time and because time seemingly is fleeting we end up with stressors in our life. Stressors in our life tend to bring about feelings of being overwhelmed and overloaded. Our responsibilities such as home, work, church, school, children, grand-children, and the list goes on combines to accentuate the stress in our life. Need I go on, now the car starts acting up, seems like you're always running a little behind and every signal light you approach is red. The clock seems to have become our enemy because no matter what happens or don't happens it just keeps on ticking. How about three months ago that family member or friend you mention you would call, come by and sit for a while. You can never have control if you don't control your time management.

The Message Bible, Proverbs 21:5 says, "Careful planning puts you ahead in the long run; hurry and scurry puts you further behind."

None of us have a time problem, we have a priority problem. You cannot be effective in time management until you honor the importance of priorities. Control is all about priorities. Being successful at time management will require work, hard work, because most of us have been out of control for such a long time.

Probably many of you know the illustration of the physics teacher who gave his students a wide-mouth mason jar. He then gave them five big rocks, a handful of marbles, a container of sand and a glass of water. He said, "You've got fifteen seconds to put these items in the jar." The physics teacher then steps back with stopwatch in hand and yelled, "Go!" The students poured in the sand, threw in the marbles and started stuffing the rocks in. After fifteen seconds, he shouted, "Times up." There still sitting on the table were three large rocks and the glass of water. The students started complaining, "It can't be done. It's impossible. All that stuff will not fit. The jar is too small."

The teacher calmly said, "I can put them all in the jar." The students responded, "Show us." So, they dumped everything back on the table, separated everything, and started over. The teacher then took the jar and placed a couple of the big rocks in the jar. He filled in any gaps around the rocks and all the marbles. The teacher then took the sand and slowly poured it into the jar and watched as it cascaded around the rocks and the marbles filling all the holes and spaces. He then took the glass of water and poured it into the jar. Everything fit perfectly and within the fifteen seconds. He then said, "It all fits but it depends on the order that you put them in the jar --- that is a matter of setting priorities. When you set priorities, you can make it happen." The Master Teacher believes in priorities He has said, "Seek first.........." When you set priorities, you will fit what's most important in and the other will not be stressful because in most cases those could wait.

Your family, your career, your business, your week, your life can and will go much better with planning. It was years before I understood what I'm sharing with you and it has been one of the largest, life-changing things I've done. Please understand this is something which will not come overnight. You will need to practice, and practice then fight the temptation to go back to your old ways. I've always said changing is much easier than 'staying' changed. When you want it bad enough you will fight for it. That's why our Maker tells us 'It's a Good Fight of Faith". If you don't plan and control your life, someone or something else will plan and control your life. Don't plan your day in the morning, plan your day the night before the day. Eventually you will begin planning your week on Sunday. It's a process, it's a journey. John Maxwell teaches and train us concerning "The Law of Process" and there is a process involved in developing and accomplishing.

John Maxwell says, "Champions don't become champions in the ring, they are merely recognized there."

It is never too late to start. I've recently decided to pursue my college career to obtain a doctorate and it might be said I'm past college age. Just recently shared that with a friend of mine who owns his own car business and he smiled at me and said, "As successful as you are you don't need to go to college." He went on to say, "Are you doing this for your ego?" I smiled and said maybe that is a little of the reason, however, I shared with him it's an accomplishment I would think about off and on now for about a year or two. I want to do it because I know I will benefit from it and make me better at everything I do or decide to do. It's a vital part of my destiny and purpose. By God's grace I have obtained a modest life with quite a few perks and it's not necessary the need for the degree at this stage of my life toward earning income, but I know for where I'm being taken and what's on the horizon, this degree will be an enormous plus.

Colonel Sanders opened his first fried chicken establishment at the fresh, youthful, and dear age of sixty. Success is not a destination; success is a journey. Personal development is on-going and continual; however, most will not even get started. It's been said the best time to start is NOW!

I have seen too many individuals controlled by their past relationships and failures. Life has dealt them a hand of cynicism and mistrust. The only solutions to undoing your past is to go back in time or move forward in this time.

"The past cannot be changed, forgotten, edited or erased; it can only be ACCEPTED."

I found many locked into their past and their conversation is about what happened to them ten or twenty years ago. I've listen as people have informed me of their present situation was due to his fault or her fault, even though it was years ago. Their past has control over them and they either don't know how or don't desire to get past it. I understand many have been seriously hurt in the past and life gives us bad experiences. Some have unforgettable and seemingly unforgiveable past hurts which they many times think no one understands. Whether someone understands or not is least of the problem which exists with the person. The problem is many haven't forgiven themselves for holding on and allowing their past to control their destiny. To forgive is not to forget, it is to never mention it again. Now that's true forgiveness. You don't have to regret your past, if there is regret it should be for the time you wasted with the wrong people, doing little, and doing nothing. Now accept that and move on.

The Apostle Paul said, "But one thing I do: Forgetting what lies behind and reaching forward to what lies ahead." Get a big enough future and you won't think much about your past. I spend hardly any seconds thinking about the ones who spoke negatively about me when I lost everything. The thought of those who I knew was hoping I didn't succeed hardly ever cross my mind now because I am so focus on where I'm going, developing myself, and reaching my God-given destiny there's no time for thinking about them nor past mistakes. Our past has given us the strength and wisdom we have today, so let's celebrate it! We cannot and will not allow our past or them to haunt us. There are so many beautiful accomplishments which lay ahead for those who believe in the beauty of their dreams. Sometimes when I'm thinking about my future it brings a huge smile to my face. I prefer smiling anytime to frowning. Doctors and scientists have found frowning produces more wrinkles in the face than smiling. When your enemy attempts to bring up your past remind him how his future looks utterly bleak. When your mind attempts to dwell on un-productive past events and people, bring every thought into captivity and think on good things.

My friend Les Brown says, "Don't let anything or anybody steal your dream."

6) CREATE

Creativity is to invent, to come up with a new way of presenting ideas, concepts and useful things.

"Life isn't about finding yourself, life is about creating yourself and in creating yourself, you will find yourself"

Recently, while listening to an Earl Nightingale recording he mention a quote by Albert Einstein in which he said, "Imagination is everything." Mr. Nightingale mentioned he wasn't the originator of that quote but he strongly believed in it, and so do I. Imagination is one of the six mental faculties we as humans have at our disposal. After childhood we tend to allow it to die.

Creative people have a way of always keeping life interesting, innovative and invigorating. Charles Schutz created the characters "Snoopy" and "Charlie Brown". Walt Disney created "Mickey and Minnie Mouse" and several others. The Bible has it written that God created the world and all that is within it.

Many are wanting to create overnight wealth instead of creating something which will bring about the wealth. We should not strive excessively to create wealth, we should strive excessively to create worth. Our personal worth creates personal wealth. We are created beings and it is part of our DNA to create. We have been designated with creative power from The Almighty. I am a firm believer that we create our own destiny by our daily choices. What we do today determines how we live later and what we acquire in life. With all respect, many Christians are sitting idly by and waiting on God to bless them with riches and wealth immensely either by hope or misunderstanding of the scriptures. Scriptures has never supported the automatic and instant wealth through faith. What my wife and I have acquired has been by the Grace of GOD, however, it didn't come overnight, it was plenty of sweat, sometimes tears, the 'never quit, never give up' mentality of hard work, persistence, and patience.

There is no Biblical support that God freely gave abundance for doing nothing. There are Scriptures which indicate such, (Deuteronomy 6, Joshua 24, Isaiah 37, Jeremiah 29), these mentions receiving from God houses you didn't build, vineyards you didn't plant, cisterns hewn out which you did not hew, but true understanding of these scriptures lend me to the thought of someone had to build, plant, and hew for it to be given away. I know of people who have received or been given just out of the kindness of someone's heart and it's by God's Grace.

I'm a strong believer in miracles, but God doesn't give miracles except for HIS Glory not ours. It is in our nature to want something for nothing, a whole lot for a little, or to get rich quick, however, the real fact of the matter is that if you want something you will need to do something and that something needs to be different than what you've been doing.

Albert Einstein said, "The height of insanity is to keep doing what you've been doing and expect something different."

The reason you can do something different is because

creation is part of your DNA. If you want more out of life you will need do more in life. If you want the best life can give, then you will need to give life your best and that only comes by you developing yourself into what God has purpose you to be. I believe in everyone's life there are three days which are critical in a person's life no matter who they are and one of those days is the day they find and/or realized their purpose. God created all of us and all of us can create. Every seed produces after its own kind. Ephesians chapter five, verses one and two says, 'Watch what God does, and then you do it, like children who learn proper behavior from their parents'. (The Bible says we are gods, Psalm 82, with a small 'g'. There is only one and true 'Big G'.)

Bangambiki Habyarimana said, "Stop searching for god in the farthest corners of the universe. He is in you. You are it."

With utter respect my belief is there is a Supreme Being which is The Creator of all. I believe we have attributes and qualities from Him. Notice how some people 'create' a life of wealth and riches? Religion has very little to do with the true and awesomeness of what we have been commissioned by God to do and carry out. We carry the power within to create a wonderful world for us, our children, and our future. The world needs your creativity. Our Creator has given us creative energies and abilities that He wants us to help humanity by those creative ideas He has given us. One of the riches places on earth is the graveyard because so many have passed on with gifts, talents, and creativity which the world never received because of fear of failing, being wrong, and slothfulness. God gave Daniel extraordinary wisdom to be creative in the way that he overcame evil with good. The king noticed Daniel's talents and Daniel's nation he was in greatly benefited from Daniel's creativity. Our Creator wants to give you creative wisdom in all your relationships, activities and personal endeavors.

To live a creative life, we must lose our fear of being wrong.

Joseph was taken out of a pit and sent to the palace over a course of time and challenges. Joseph found himself sitting at the right hand of the most powerful person in kingdom and ask to come up with a plan to help save the kingdom. With wisdom and the Grace of God he created a program which not only saved the kingdom but gave abundance in later years during a famine which allowed others to benefit. Creativity is something you are gifted with for the benefit of others and you. Again, just as Daniel, the nation which Joseph was a part of was greatly blessed by the creativity of Joseph. Not to mention the warm and fuzzy feeling one acquires when he or she helps someone else.

The desire to create is one of the deepest yearnings of the human soul. You will need to create motivation within yourself on occasions. The Bible shares with us how King David encouraged himself. It is always good to hear someone encouraging and motivating as often as possible, not to mention, I would rather be around people of motivation than people which are non-motivated. Some people don't believe in motivation and that may be fine for them, but most people could use some motivation if their goal is to accomplish more than just what the masses do. Motivation is like a bath or shower; a person should not go a day or two without. Motivation is the fuel necessary to keep the human engine running. Success comes before work only in the dictionary and motivation will keep you working toward your success.

You must understand true success comes by working hard, focus, and persistence. So many people have perished because they don't have a vision or dream of what they desire out of life. The first step to success is to create in your mind a vision for what you would desire out of your life. Many years ago, I met a ninth grade educated millionaire who helped me immensely by mentoring me and teaching me how to find my 'why'. His story was that at the level of ninth grade he quit school and started working. Of course, many years later into his adulthood he met a professor from MIT, his destiny evolved, they worked together in a multi-level type business, and became rather wealthy. Now go figure this, a guy who dropped out of school in the ninth grade and a professor who graduated from one of the most prestigious engineering institution of our time working together. You never know who God will bring into your life once you decide to develop yourself.

I have a chapter in my first best-selling book, 'You Can Win in Life', a chapter entitle, "When the Student Is Ready, The Teacher Will Appear". It tells the story of how I met this ninth grade educated millionaire through another guy whom I met one eventful day in a grocery store. Here is the question which helped me find my 'why'. This is what was asked of me, "C. Ray if money wasn't an issue in your life, what would you do?" I paused and replied to him, "Wow, I don't know, I had never thought about that." Currently in my life I had been working several years, raising a family, and working my fingers to the bone to get my first business endeavor off the ground. Worked two jobs at one time and realized two jobs are for two people. Cost me twice as much in gas, automobile maintenance, and time which ultimately equated to not much difference in my income development. I submit to you, the very clear majority of people whom have experienced life like mine, working and paying bills, have never thought about the question which had asked me because what we are earning yearly will never allow us to think about the answer to that question. Now that you have been made aware of that question what would be your answer? Don't just blurt out the first thing that pops in your mind, dwell on the question for a moment, then consider your words while saying what you believe you would do. If you desire to accomplish something of significance which will be a blessing, not only to you but to your family also, your answers to that question should be about others, helping others, and/or making a difference in someone else's life. A portion of my answer was inclusive of being in a position where as my spouse would not necessarily have a need to be employed for financial resources. When your answer has abandoned selfishness and any part of it you are on your way to fine-tuning your 'why'. When the 'why' is big enough, the how doesn't matter any longer. You will find a how when your 'why' becomes large enough in your heart.

The Dalai Lama said, "Our prime purpose in this life is to help others. And if you can't help them, at least don't hurt them."

The Creator will give you the desires of your heart and when we read that it does not mean automatic. It means with the proper procedures practiced and performed each day you will acquire the desires of your heart.

As I've mention earlier we are to imitate Our Father and the Bible doesn't specifically say what to imitate and what not to imitate. If there are no do's and don'ts, then what my Father did I can do. There is no reference which says The Creator did this, but you can't. Please understand not to the degree of what The Creator has or does but certainly we have been initiated with levels of imitation permitted by God. God created the world and we can create a world of ours. God created man and woman, thusly, we can create a new man and new woman by the born-again experience. When we become new it causes others to become new which means we created a new person. Now if you can believe the possibilities of your creative power and abilities then you can create the world you desire.

> **What you think, you become.**
> **What you feel, you attract.**
> **What you imagine, you create.**

We lived in a neighborhood of low income families and I decided to create a better environment for my children. I worked hard to build my business and we could move out of that neighborhood in Dallas and move into a neighborhood in Desoto, a suburb of Dallas, which was predominantly of a different ethnicity. This exposure was a positive influence in our lives and the lives of our children. They were around a different type of atmosphere and environment. People are no better than one another, however, how they think, talk, and live can be somewhat different and better. In his book, Rich Dad, Poor Dad, author Robert Kiyosaki details how the wealthy live and talk different than the poor. His rich dad was his best friend's father who was uneducated but had his own business and the poor dad was Robert's biological father who had earned a master's Degree. He writes in his book the conversations and how different they were at the dinner table of his own family and the family of his best friend. With all due respect, it is not the ethnicity or economic condition of individuals which makes a person better than the next, it is one's heart which makes the difference. People are better when they choose to better themselves and make a difference in other's lives. We are not to be in competition with anyone other than ourselves from the day before. Most want a better life and that's inclusive of an increase in one's finances, however, many don't realize the more you develop your 'worth' the more your 'wealth' will develop. There is a direct correlation between the two.

> *"If you don't use today to better yourself;*
> *what do you need tomorrow for?"*

One of the most powerful keys to creating your desired world is to get control of your tongue. It is your words which create or destroys. Your words condemn or justify. Your words are what shapes your world and brings about your future. God spoke, and it came into existence. For us to imitate our Father we must speak also, and it will become. Whether you believe it or not does not negate the truth of this fact, you can and will have what you say. We have the creative power to call things which are not, and it will come into existence.

Another key in the developments in my growth was to change what went into my mind, thusly, changing what came out of my mouth. For your words have a direct correlation to what's in your mind. It is imperative you begin to renew your mind and develop the mindset of the successful. It is a true statement that when you change your thinking, your life must change. It is impossible to change your thinking and your life does not change. When I challenge my clients and listeners to read I informed them to read books of substance in the categories of self-help, consulting, millionaires mindsets, and books of the kind. You can read romance novels, but they won't get you where you need to be or where you need to go. Your growth is a needed necessity in your world, your family, and your future. Don't allow yourself the satisfaction of not improving and developing because out of it will come life changing results you will be proud of. I look back over where I've come from and I am so overjoyed with what life has given me when I give life my best up to this point because the best is yet to come.

Many people are 'hung by their tongue'. Your words bring about a result and the result can be good, not so good, or bad. Practice saying something nice every day and if you are already doing that then step it up a notch or two. One kind word can change someone's entire day. Kind words are a creative force, a power that concurs in the building up of all that is good, and energy that showers blessings upon the world. Kind words do not cost much, however, yet they accomplish much. Proverbs sixteen, twenty-four says, "Kind words are like honey; sweet to the soul and healthy for the body." When you live intentionally each day to make someone's world a little bit better you are creating a better world for yourself.

Abraham Lincoln said, "The best way to predict your future is to create it."

Creating your future of success and abundance starts when you decide today this is it, wake up to a realization, my world can and will be better. As I speak, nationally and internationally, I constantly and consistently inform all if you want a greater success the next year don't wait to make a new year's resolution because that is too late for that year. Your next year success depends on what you do this year. It is amazing how many people I meet who inform me of them getting started soon. Soon never comes to get started for anything. There's an old cliché which says, "Why put off tomorrow that what can be done today." The only better time to start than now is yesterday. Since yesterday is gone then 'now' is the time to start.

"The future is not something we enter;
The future is something we create."

You may have made some mistakes, and you may not be where you want to be, but that's got nothing to do with your future, if, and when, you decide to create it. Along the way you will discover gifts and talents you never knew you possess. The real you are an exceptional individual with qualities your family and your friends need. If a person could see their future choices based on what they do daily they would see the best future is the one which daily they did something which cause them to come out of their comfort zone.

"A comfort zone is a beautiful place, but nothing ever grows there."

7) C's DISEASE

"Complaining is finding faults. Wisdom is finding solutions."

Be careful through life many have been infected with the three C's disease and it has stifle the accomplishments of many. The dreaded three C's disease is Complaining, Criticizing, and Condemning.

I have come to recognize the negative effect complaining brings to a situation. The Greek word translated "complainer" means literally "one who is discontented with his or her lot in life." Complaining and blaming other people doesn't help anything and makes you miserable company. Complaining is not listed in the fruit of the Spirit and it is detrimental to one's peace, joy, and patience. Complaining is destructive and debilitating personally and only serves to make life more difficult. I have found this to be true, when you complain, life gives you more to complain about. Have you noticed people who complain excessively don't attract too many friends? It is imperative to develop a renewed mind and one of the attributes to a positive mindset is the realization that complaining works little to none productivity. Those who have a positive attitude on life tend not to complain about it.

A positive attitude is said to be everything and that has some validity to it. If it's not everything then it is the most important thing. I cannot express how important and vital having a positive attitude is in reaching your God-given destiny. God would not allow complainers to enter the land of more than enough and that God is still the same, yesterday, today, and forever. When I say positive attitude I'm not talking about walking around day by day as if you are floating on a cloud and nothing bad is never going to happen. I mean being a person who sees the best, believes the best, and strives for the best in all things. Understanding that life will have its ups and downs, but it will never keep me down and a positive attitude knows this. I have never seen a complainer become an overcomer. Complaining is a person's way of saying he or she is always right. Most complainers are not happy people because they are always finding something to complain about. Happiness comes when we stop complaining about the troubles we have and offer thanks for all the troubles we don't have. It's easy to complain and many times not difficult to resolve what one is complaining about. We need only to take the energy we used to complain with and use that energy to find the solution even if it meant us taking on the responsibility to rectify it.

In our organizations, I teach all the leaders to bring a solution to the table with the complaint. No solution, no complaints. If you spend five minutes complaining without a recommendation or solution you have just wasted five minutes we cannot get back.

There is so much good and productivity which one can perform in the place of complaining. Suggest to me a possible avenue of solving. Tell me something you love or love to do. Tell me something you appreciate or someone who you would love to do something for. Tell me something that makes you smile or causes you to laugh out loud. Here's my point, when you want to complain think about the things which will cause you not to.

Jean Ferris said, "I know it's important to do more than just complain when there's something you don't like. You need to try to do something about it, or you're nothing but a whiner."

Many people complain many times a day to our families, friends, co-workers, customer service representatives, and even strangers in the elevator. Some people go out of their way to find someone to listen to their complaints. Several studies have showed when some individual voice complaints regularly it can have huge implications on one's mental health. This knowledge revealed through the study also includes negative physical implications.

In our modernistic world and our daily lives more than ever in history we find reasons and/or excuses to complain not realizing rarely does complaining bring about the results we would prefer. Invariably many regularly find themselves repeating the same sad tale of dissatisfaction to one person after the other in effort to rid themselves of their frustration. One reason I informed many of the necessity to not rehearse, repeatedly the issue which has you complaining, is each time it's mention the frustration and aggravation is relived over again and again. I've always believed negativity and complaining is detrimental to our health and state of mind.

Recently during my reading, I found this article by Psychology Today and I begin to shake my head as I read it. The article went on to report, "The problem is that today we associate the act of complaining with venting far more than we do with problem solving. Thus, we complain simply to get things off our chest, not to resolve problems or to create change, rendering most of our complaints completely ineffective. Even when we do address our complaints to the people who can do something about them, we tend to be unsuccessful far often. Take a moment to consider how many things you complain about in each day. The weather, public transportation and traffic, your spouse, your kids, your friends, your boss, the movie you just saw and hated, the meal that arrived cold in the restaurant, the sandwich shop that got your order wrong, the elevator that took too long, the reality television show that booted off your favorite contestant, and the list goes on and on. When we have so many dissatisfactions and frustrations yet believe we're powerless to do much about them or to get the results we want, we are left feeling helpless, hopeless, victimized, and bad about ourselves. Obviously, one such incident won't harm our mental health, but we have so many complaints, this scenario happens many times a day. This accumulation of frustration and helplessness can add up over time and impact our mood, our self-esteem, and even our general mental health."

The article went on to say there is a way to effectively complain and how it can have an empowering effect on our mood and self-esteem. Before reading this article I personally had never heard of the terminology effective complaining. If there is an issue, I call voice my complaint, I keep a positive attitude causing a positive atmosphere and usually proceed to getting it amicably resolve. Now I know I just effectively complain. (LOL)

However, if you take one hundred people who address an unpleasant issue, ninety-nine of them usually don't effectively complain. I've talked with many individuals who perform customer related service for companies and I have never heard in conversations with them, (and there have been many), of customers expressing effective complaints. I've heard of threats, profanity, hollering and/or screaming, hanging up the phone in their face, and the like. Here's my point, the fact of the matter is very clear, most people do not effectively complain.

Maya Angelou said, "What you're supposed to do when you don't like a thing is change it. If you can't change it change the way you think about it. Don't complain."

George Sand said, "God abandons only those who abandon themselves and whoever has the courage to shut up his sorrow within his own heart is stronger to fight against it than he who complains."

Now that we have come to the realization we are not complaining any more let's move on to the next step of self-improvement. Second to the disease of complaining is criticism. My number one best-selling book, 'You Can Win in Life' has numerous reviews, I'm honored and humbled by the many kind words which many have written about the book. I must confess there is one bad review concerning the book. When I was thrust into the limelight by the book going to number one status in two categories I was all smiles and happy. As I read the reviews smiling I read the bad review and this person criticize the book and gave it one-star rating. I started feeling a little bit uneasy. I started thinking who they think they are. I thought about seeking this person, find out how I could get a message to this person, and send a very nice, to the point, message.

Then suddenly I came to myself and begin to laugh. One of my favorite quotes when I'm speaking to audiences is that anything in motion causes friction. Why should I spend anytime dwelling on this person's opinion? My friend, Les Brown says, what they person thinks about me is none of MY business. I need to emphasize so far concerning reviews on my book there is ONE negative critic. Allow me to say that again......ONE! The book with that one-star rating is still sitting at 4.5-star rating because of the other great reviews. That critic does not have a best-selling book by the way.

Your success will bring false friends and true enemies. I started smiling because that negative review is what successful people must endure because critics are a dime a dozen, no a nickel a dozen, and they are your sign you are moving up in life and being recognized. There are no statues erected for critics. I would consider it being constructive criticism if there were one or two others. When one hundred pat you on the back and just one point a critical finger at you I encourage you to utilize my 'water off a duck's back' philosophy. A duck is created with a natural coating on their wings which causes water to roll or slide off leaving them the ability to still fly after coming from under water. When you are criticized just let it 'roll off your back', stay focus, and continue doing what you know is right.

Most criticism is an easy form of ego defense. Many people are not pleased with others success and develop a 'hating' spirit. We don't criticize because we disagree with a behavior or an attitude. We criticize because we somehow feel devalued by the person, the person's behavior, attitude, and/or accomplishments. Critical people tend to be easily insulted and especially in need of ego defense. – Psychology Today

"Criticism is the only reliable form of autobiography," Oscar

Wilde said, because it tells you more about the psychology of the critic than the people he or she criticizes. Astute professionals can formulate a viable diagnostic hypothesis just from hearing someone's criticisms.

Dale Carnegie, author of many books and one of my favorites, 'How to Win Friends and Influence People', writes, "Any fool can criticize, complain, and condemn----and most fools do. But it takes character and self-control to be understanding and forgiving."

Many well-meaning parents have caused an inferior complex upon their children because of criticism. It is imperative for us to move away from the disease of criticism and become an encourager. Adults have behavior issues during their adulthood because someone criticized them at home and/or at school in their youth. Low self-esteem has been a product of criticism, as well as, a person's potential being stifle because someone criticized them for attempting to do something or be something. When you criticize, you focus on what's wrong instead of focusing on how to improve what's wrong. When you criticize many times, the person wants control or is attempting to gain control and does not respect the right(s) of others. When you criticize, you are placing the blame on someone else and you should be focusing on the future and making it better. When you criticize, you are devaluing others and you should be adding value as often as you can. Criticism is to your relationship what smoking is to your health. When a critical person refuses to, or does not, absolutely get a handle on their impulse to criticize, it carries the potential to ruin relationships, draw enemies, and cease them from reaching their God-given destiny.

"Be an encourager; The world has plenty of critics already."

Student says, "I am very discouraged. What should I do? Master says, "Encourage others."

The word encourage comes from the Old French word encoragier, meaning "make strong, hearten." Many don't know or realize the Greek word for "encourage," parakaleo, appears one hundred and five times in the New Testament. Somehow, encouragement has become confused with complimenting or praising others. While praise can be part of encouragement, it doesn't cover the full meaning of the word. We often think of encouragement as saying nice things to others to make them feel good about themselves, but this is closer to the definition of a compliment. Encouraging someone can mean you're giving them support or confidence but is also means that you're helping to develop something in them. When you encourage someone, you give him or her the courage or confidence to do something or be something, like encouraging your brother or sister to play harder by yelling their name from the sidelines.

When the Bible talks about encouragement, it usually means that one is calling someone to their side to teach, comfort, strengthen or push them to act in a certain way. There are a few other words in the Bible that have similar meaning, such as exhort, warn or admonish, but they are mostly used in Paul's letters. People who encourage others say with love what a person needs to hear, when they need to hear it–even if it isn't what the person wants to hear.

If encouraging is not much a part of your persona, work at becoming one, and start encouraging others because your words may be the only pillars of strength for someone who is pulling themselves up to stand again and your words will give them something to lean on. I cannot count the times I have been informed concerning something I said to someone during a trying time in their life and I was told how those words helped them immensely. John Maxwell says a leader knows the way, goes the way, and shows the way. I would like to add when you are a good leader your actions will inspire others to dream more, learn more, do more, and become more.

I personally know some individuals who are gifted in the arena of encouraging. There are some who may not do it often but when they encourage you, like my wife Peggy, it is an awesome, uplifting, and always at the right time. When I was going through some of the toughest times in my life she could, when I was least expecting it, say an encouraging word which would be so timely and powerful I would move into my next level of accomplishment. John Currie, my brother in law, is one who embodies the gift of encouragement. Five minutes with him and you feel like you were just featured on lifestyles of the rich and famous. He doesn't have to work at it because he shares with me how he remembers when we needed encouragement many times and did not get it. What would this world be if there were countless others who spent much of their day encouraging others? I enjoy being around that brother in law and people like him.

On a regular basis I meet with our local law enforcement department to assist them and sometime train in areas of leadership and cultural differences. I am not employed by them but after I completed a domestic abuse certification program, with background check, I now assist them concerning domestic violence and abuse throughout the city. We have formed a group of clergy and police in our city,

DeSoto Police and Clergy, also known as DPAC. The clergy carry on as Ministers on Call, (MOC), as we respond to domestic abuse and violence alongside the police and minister to those which have been abused. Recently I was asked by the police chief to speak at their annual retreat for his leadership which was the captains, sergeants, and lieutenants. I was training, speaking, and encouraging from the content of leadership, teamwork, cultural differences, and how most of the community really appreciate our law enforcement department. One week later one officer in another meeting said to the group, "We need to keep him (me) around all the time. He perks everyone up." People identifies with an encourager, want to be around them, and want them around. Anyone can tear down, but it makes life worth living when you lift others up.

I speak to youth groups all over the country and their leaders inform me that one of the reasons I'm requested so often is my humor and my ability to make them believe dreams can come true. I love to meet the young people, ask what grade they're in, and what will they be when they graduate college. I always encourage and tell them what a great 'whatever' they are going to be. To see their eyes light up, to see their demeanor glisten gives me a warm, fuzzy, feeling inside that maybe I planted a seed of destiny in them.

The movie Pay It Forward, starring Kevin Spacey, is not so far-fetched. That person you encourage can change the world by following your lead. We should challenge ourselves to find a way to encourage someone on a regular basis each day. Encouraging someone is a one good way to 'pay it forward'.

I am a strong believer in the fact that if someone will condemn and gossip to you about others; they will condemn and gossip to others about you.

The third leg of the three C's disease is condemning, and it will cause you to fall well short of any beneficial goal you have set. The path to a successful life will never come to fruition when a spirit of condemnation exists in a person. Webster defines condemn as expressing complete disapproval of someone or something. Most condemnation comes from prejudices of people thinking different, looking different, and having different ideologies.

Malcolm X said, "Don't be in a hurry to condemn because someone doesn't do what you do or think as you think or as fast. There was a time when you didn't know what you know today."

While finishing up this book two days overdue from my goal of completion I find myself watching the seventh game of the World Series, in the bottom of the tenth inning, and it is one of the best baseball games I have witnessed that I can remember. Last year watching my favorite team, the Kansas City Royals, down two runs come from behind in the ninth inning to tie the game against the Mets, and ultimately winning it in the twelfth. However, that was the fifth and final game as KC won the series four games to one. The Royals were destined to win because the year before they lost the World Series and 2015 was a team on a mission to accomplish the victory. Oh, by the way, the game I'm watching just ended in the tenth inning and the Chicago Cubs won. I wanted the Cubs to win since they had not won a World Series since 1908, one hundred and eight years. Seventh game extra innings in the pinnacle baseball game, the World Series, will always overshadow a fifth game win in the World Series.

I begin writing about the teams because of their encouraging nature and commitment to one another every play, every hit, every miss, and it did not matter they encourage one another continuously. We are to be the same way in our everyday life. Life is not so much about what you get, it's more about what you give. If someone miss catching a ball or pitcher threw a bad pitch and gave up a homerun there are always encouraging. There is no condemnation no matter what mistake was or is made. The athletic world is more encouraging than the world of Christianity, seemingly. Reminds me of the Bible stating there is no condemnation upon us and certainly we have no right to place condemnation on others. People who readily condemn others usually do so because they don't like themselves very much, and therefore feel the need to bring others down so that they can feel superior to them.

Carl Jung said, "We cannot change anything until we accept it. Condemnation does not liberate, it oppresses."

"Therefore encourage one another and build each other up, just as in fact you are doing."
1_ Thessalonians 5:11

8) CONQUEROR

A conqueror is a person who conquers a place or people; to gain or acquire by force of arms; to overcome by force of arms; to gain mastery over or win by overcoming obstacles or opposition; to overcome by mental or moral power.

Most people define 'more than conquerors' as conquering completely and absolutely. Webster's dictionary gives a similar meaning somewhat like what most people define 'more than conquerors'. If that is true, then there would be no need to say, 'more than'. To me personally the biblical statement of 'more than' emphasizing more than what many clergy and Webster's definition states. If the Apostle Paul extend the definition of conquering to 'more than', to me it's obvious the Apostle's 'more than conquerors' carries a different and more definitive meaning than just a conqueror.

More than conquerors signify to me that we are not only victorious in our personal lives, but we carry the ability to transform other's lives and circumstances into victories, proving to them the power and glory of God. More than conquerors through love will result in converting enemies into friends, obstacles into opportunities, and problems into solutions. Now that's more than just conquering and you winning in life. I read where a respected pastor gave an illustration of what the meaning of 'More than Conquerors' was. He used the illustration of a boxer who fought hard and won a prize in a boxing match. The boxer went home and gave the prize to his wife. His wife was the "more than conqueror" because she received all the benefits and the prize from all the practice, extensive training, and all the painful hard work he put in to acquire the prize. Though this being a nice illustration of 'more than conqueror' I feel the need to carry it a bit further. A conqueror overcomes the enemy by confrontation and force like Webster's meaning defines. 'More than' indicates to me the realization of overcoming the enemy not by my strength but by someone else's victory which is given to me. But that's not all, 'more than conqueror' entails not only overcoming the enemy but converting the enemy to become friends by acts of love. Notice the scriptures states, "No, in all these things we are more than conquerors through HIM who loved us. It said 'In' which indicates when we are in trouble, hardship, persecution, famine, nakedness, danger, or sword we have the 'more than' because of Him to endure, grow, sustain, and come through as pure gold because He has given us the victory. When you complain, you remain. You must see yourself in every situation as a 'more than' and eventually you will become what you see yourself as.

Denis Waitley said, "It's not what you are that holds you back, it's what you think you are not."

God is the Great I Am, and HIS children are the great 'you are'. You are what you chose to be. I once had a severe stuttering impediment and when it was seemingly impossible I started telling myself 'YOU ARE' a great speaker and communicator. Thusly, I become what my mind and the world said was impossible. It began with me thinking it and saying it. You can do all things through HIM! The ability to change your destiny begins with a renewed mind.

Psychologist William James said, "The greatest discovery of my generation is that human beings can alter their lives by altering their attitude of mind. If you can change your mind, you can change your life."

Here this is a guy, William James, whose life was the study of human behavior, the choices of success, as well as, the choices of failures. He spent his life studying the principles and laws of living which govern the results of human behavior. Mr. James states a person can change his or her life by altering the thought process. Your mind is the catalyst to you being 'more than' and living a victorious life of winning.

It is human nature to be fearful especially facing insurmountable odds of opposition. There are many illustrations in the Bible of God bringing miraculous victory to HIS people. Humanly speaking, we are no match for much of what we face, but God always tell us to 'not be afraid', that HE would fight our battles for us. One must understand the writing on the wall; HE fights our battles for us, through us. There will always come all kinds of life-defeating, joy-stealing attacks to threaten our faith and well-being. To be more than conquerors means we face the trials and tests of life with the certainty that we are not alone. We approach all obstacles, darkest valleys, and doubtful circumstances with the certainty that we are never alone.

Not long ago I did a five-week Mastermind Class session using the content from John Maxwell's book entitle, The 15 Invaluable Laws of Growth. The first law we studied and discussed was The Law of Intentionality which simply states growth doesn't just happen. The kind of growth we're speaking of is the development of one's totality into the person The Creator has called you to be and/or become. I periodically hold Mastermind Group session which allows participants to bring fresh ideas and individual perspective to the sessions. These facilitated by me group sessions offer a combination of masterminding, peer brainstorming, education, accountability, and support in a group setting to sharpen your business and personal skills. By bringing fresh ideas and a different perspective, my masterminds can help you achieve success in any and every area of one's life.

Having been certified and trained by the John Maxwell Team, (and we continue to be trained and taught by John and the team), we assist in developing people so that they will have the best chance of becoming the person they were created to be. Our perspective on growth and leadership is everything rises and falls on leadership. A leader knows the way, goes the way, and shows the way. It's all about personal growth and development. To be the person you have been created to be and to do the things you were created to do you must be intentional about your personal growth. We should and can be 'can do' people. We've been told what not to do, what we can't do so much and so long, we failed to grab hold of all the things we can do. You must realize you are unstoppable. There is a force inside of you which is your potential and when tapped into correctly makes you greater than any outward force. If anybody told you it would be easy, then they will probably lie about other things too.

Tony Robbins says, "In essence, if we want to direct our lives, we must take control of our consistent actions. It's not what we do once in a while that shapes our lives, but what we do consistently."

It is our consistent behavior which dictate our conclusion. After I lost just about all I had and found myself homeless, hopeless, and sitting in a local hotel room on the edge of the bed with suicidal thoughts from depression, a small still voice inside spoke to me, rest and tomorrow this is what you will do. I begin seeing myself as a 'more than' conqueror and start saying to myself repeatedly positive affirmations. I continued this day in and day out. I would not allow my thoughts to slip back to negative and detrimental memories of what was lost. I brought every thought which did not align with what God said about me into captivity and spoke health, wealth, and prosperity. Here's my point, you must see yourself and be yourself which is what The Creator said you were, right now and consistently. Then you will move from where you are to where you should be. Where you should be is ahead and not beneath. Now when others see what has happen in my life it inspires them to believe it's possible for them to achieve their dreams, goals, and aspirations.

Success isn't just about what you accomplish in your life; It's about what you inspire others to do.

Johann Wolfgang von Goethe said, "Correction does much, but encouragement does more."

It is a hidden value to give up what you may think is good, so you can receive what's best. The best of life is many times kept from many because they 'think' they are doing okay. Respectfully, they may be doing okay but there is always something better.

When life birth pain it can also at the same time birth purpose.

Life is known to birth hurtful pain and from pain can come purpose, behind purpose comes passion, behind passion comes power, and behind power comes provisions. The Bible says life birth Job much pain causing him to lose it all but after all was said and done Job received double for his trouble. Elisha ask for a difficult thing to do, asking his mentor for a double portion of 'can do' anointing so he could do twice as much and because he was present when his mentor departed he received what he ask and accomplish twice the miracles of his predecessor. Gideon had such low self-esteem but begin to believe in himself and when he arrived back at the camp just in time to hear a man telling his friend about his dream his friend responded, "This can be nothing other than the sword of Gideon, son of Joash, the Israelite. God has given the Midianites and the whole camp into his hands. "When Gideon heard the dream and its interpretation, he bowed down and worshiped. He returned to the camp of Israel and called out, "Get up! The Lord has given the Midianites camp into your hands." Gideon defeated an enormous army of men with three hundred soldiers. C. Ray lost just about all he had, from drug, alcohol addiction, trouble with the law, and suicidal thoughts rose to becoming a best-selling author, entrepreneur and owner of several businesses, to Certified Coach, Speaker, Trainer, and Teacher with the John Maxwell Team, working with law enforcement agencies, training, teaching leadership, and cultural differences. If Job, Elisha, Gideon, C. Ray, and so many others could and can do it, YOU CAN TOO! God is not a respecter of persons, HE will work alongside of you when you decide, begin to step your way toward your eternal destiny which is a life of abundance and more than enough.

I like this translation from the Message Bible of this verse found in Second Corinthians by one of my favorite heroes of all time, the Apostle Paul.

The Message Bible translation of Second Corinthians, chapter eleven, the Apostle Paul says, "(I can't believe I'm saying these things. It's crazy to talk this way! But I started, and I'm going to finish.) I've worked much harder, been jailed more often, beaten up more times than I can count, and at death's door time after time. I've been flogged five times with the Jews' thirty-nine lashes, beaten by Roman rods three times, pummeled with rocks once. I've been shipwrecked three times and immersed in the open sea for a night and a day. In hard traveling year in and year out, I've had to ford rivers, fend off robbers, struggle with friends, struggle with foes. I've been at risk in the city, at risk in the country, endangered by desert sun and sea storm, and betrayed by those I thought were my brothers. I've known drudgery and hard labor, many a long and lonely night without sleep, many a missed meal, blasted by the cold, naked to the weather. And that's not half of it, when you throw in the daily pressures and anxieties of all the churches. When someone gets to the end of his rope, I feel the desperation in my bones. When someone is duped into sin, and an angry fire burns in my gut. If I have to "brag" about myself, I'll brag about the humiliations that make me like Jesus."

Many of us would have quit and many have but not this guy. He personifies the title Apostle and the guy went on to pen nearly two thirds of the New Testament with faith, encouraging words, direction, and strength! That's a WOW!

9) CONFIDENCE

What is confidence?

It is the state of feeling certain about the truth of something: Confidence is a feeling of self-assurance arising from one's appreciation of one's own abilities or qualities:

I would like to stress the importance of building your confidence in yourself. Notice the meaning of the word, it's appreciation of your own self. Confidence is your key to a successful life. Confidence is not merely a term, but it is a set of beliefs that you have in yourself. It determines how you perceive yourself and what you think you are capable of.

The Bible says to not think too highly of yourself than you ought. Notice what it did not say, it did not say not to think highly of yourself, it said not to think too highly of yourself. It did not say not to think of yourself as being an excellent creation. I've noticed in life people will start thinking too highly of themselves when they perceive they are better off than the next person. Maybe they have a nicer car or nice home than someone and they begin to move into pride which God hates. What a person possesses has nothing at all to do with a person being better than the next person. Your worth rises when others worth rises with you.

One of the basic reasons why so many people are under-confident is that they have gone through many negative things and disappointments in their life. Therefore, they hardly believe in themselves anymore. Fortunately, the solution to regain confidence is simple, but may be difficult to implement. I cannot reiterate enough the vital importance of a mind renewing program. You just need to replace these negative beliefs with positive affirmations; you must change your mind-set. You must start to believe you can do all things, start saying these types of biblical truths and affirmations on a regular basis. This is a sort of reprogramming of your mind at both conscious and subconscious levels. If done correctly, the method of positive affirmations is one of the most powerful and practical methods ever devised. One of the best programs you need to do is repeat positive affirmations for 7 to 10 min every night. How earnestly do people say they want to succeed and have a better life, yet when they have instructions on ways to succeed they don't have the endurance to continue.

The Bible says, "Therefore do not throw away your confidence, which has a great reward. For you have need of endurance, so that when you have done the will of God you may receive what is promised."

As you keep on doing your positive affirmations for a few days, it will become a habit, and within a short time, you will start noticing positive and better things happening in your life. Confidence thinking is really the mastery of one's mind. You need to have control over your thoughts and not the other way around. Once you gain this skill, and it is just a skill you develop, you then not only think positively, you'll have an aura of complete confidence and inner peace. It's your thought patterns which have the greatest impact on your life. Think about it. If you think everything in your world is horrible and that there's no hope, then how can you possibly change your life for the better? Your negative thoughts now completely control your life. The good news is that you can change this simply by learning a few techniques to gain mastery over your thoughts. You start by paying attention to your thoughts. What is that little voice you have in your head saying to you over and over? Once you start hearing these thoughts, you're going to want to know "How do I stop the negative thoughts in my head" and "How do I gain control over how I automatically react to certain situations? There are no questions you ask yourself that millions of people have not ask themselves. There's always answers but you must be willing to seek out, explore, find the right answers, and implement them in your life if you want to be the head and not the tail, the lender and not the borrower.

Sylvia Plath said, "The worst enemy to creativity is self-doubt."

Many are consumed with self-doubt which can be crippling but also devastating in that it can prevent you from your life full potential. When a person has self-doubt, it opens the door for other destiny crippling effects. Self-doubt effects your ability to handle stress in a way which won't leave you feeling overwhelmed often. A confident individual handles stress more effectively because they learn and develop stress reducing skills which cause them to react instead of choosing. People that choose are hoping their choice is right or just guessing most of the time. A person who reacts calmly, with wisdom, can analyze the stressful situation, plan which reduces or eliminates the stress factor involved.

Being confident is a mindset – it is about the way you think. It is very important to know how to build self-confidence, if you want to build your own key to success and be confident in life. Having high confidence levels means having positive thoughts and building feelings of confidence, worthiness and high regard for yourself. Individuals with high levels of confidence feel good about themselves and think positively. They feel a sense of belonging and protection. They respect themselves, appreciate others and began to build something good for themselves. They tend to be successful in life because they feel self-confident in taking on challenges, finding positive solutions, running the risk of failure to accomplish what they want, and build on the solid foundations they have made. They have even more energy to build and enjoy healthy pursuits since their energy is not lost on negative thoughts, unfavorable feelings, sensations of inability or striving to look after or please others at the expense of their own self.

One must acquire and/or build on their self-confidence reservoir. There can be many factors the reservoir of confidence which you have relies on – how you were raised, where you were raised, the relationships you acquired from your youth to adulthood, parental attitudes, life experiences, and so on. In some cases, people lose self-esteem and feel bad about themselves because of failures, dissatisfactions, and/or because of the way others in their lives have treated them in the past. It is very important to know that anyone can build his or her own confidence levels up and build a successful outlook at any time. Preferably, healthy conditioning would have taken place in childhood; however, many people discover that they must build their own levels to be confident later in life to find the solutions they desire.

To be successful you must improve your levels of self-esteem. The rewards of knowing and implementing ways of how to build confidence and self-esteem are immeasurable.

You can train yourself how to be confident with an outlook on life which will include knowing you have the resilience to overcome challenges, setbacks, and build healthy relationships. Your newfound confidence will not allow you to be kept back by self-defeating thoughts, insecurities, and fears. You will have confidence to pursue your dreams and desires, having a high level of self-belief, faith and trust, so you make good choices to reach your objectives by finding solutions to challenges.

Positive thinking helps you stop listening to your inner critic and fosters useful positive solutions in changing negative thoughts, detrimental behaviors and replacing them with favorable ones that will build levels of self-esteem. Those who have developed low self-esteem must first realize and recognize the symptoms. It is a common belief that not being confident is caused, in part, by negative emotional responses and many negative thoughts. Also, criticism, teasing, punishment and abuse, poverty, economic deprivation, failure in school and many other factors affect our feelings of how we believe about ourselves and cause people to not be confident in their decision making when it comes to finding solutions to their problems.

Rather, the process of building confidence becomes a self-fulfilling, motivating move in the right direction, and to not build your confidence is so often detrimental to your amazing God-given destiny.

Even race, religion, the media, culture and sex have an influence on our belief system and how we feel about ourselves. If we learn how to have belief, faith, trust and be confident in ourselves, finding solutions is easy. However, when negative thoughts and feelings take root early in life, they can build powerful thought patterns that form habits of thinking and become an inner critic. I remember when I started my first business how often I talked myself out of accomplishments because of lack of confidence in my own ability to perform. Before long, we begin to think in ways that limit our growth, belief, faith, trust and self-confidence. We begin to doubt ourselves and feel dissatisfied then we are unable to build anything substantial in life. We listen to our inner critic and become afraid to find solutions to challenges and feel unworthy, many times even when we do accomplish important things. The deeper these negative belief issues take root, the lower our self-esteem falls, until we cannot envision what it is like to feel inner self-confidence and to have trust and belief in all we can do.

Courage is necessary to have strength, for strength without self-confidence is useless.

Just as a person can have or acquire high confidence one can possess low confidence as well. Not being confident is sometimes hidden by other behaviors used to compensate for the deeper rooted, more painful feelings we wish to avoid. Psychologists tell us that low confidence often masks itself under a false front of superiority, perfectionism, over self-reliance, kindness or humility, arrogant or attention-seeking behavior, hyper-critical behavior or religious fanaticism.

Most people whom attend church have confidence in God and little to no confidence in themselves. They fail to realize the potential and power within themselves. These behavior patterns are meant to shield us from the underlying feelings of sadness, inferiority, fear or insecurity, and failures. They allow us to compensate for these unacceptable or painful feelings by giving us a false sense of being okay or right or better than those around us, but they are not long-term solutions – we need to build a better belief system and foundation in our lives. It is necessary to look inside our own memories. It is in our own memories that faith and trust can become emotionally embedded. When it comes to storage and retrieval of memory, in response to a given event, there may be an emotional bias towards negative faith, belief and trust in our own ability to be positive. What tends to happen is that a conservatism bias is created where previous experience and memory dictates the reaction to a present day new experience.

There is a need, here, to update our belief system – for most, this takes place slowly. The obvious solution here is to take small steps to build our own self belief system. I am a strong believer in finding solutions and there are solutions to ways to become confident. Being confident or having low self-esteem tends to develop from childhood by building patterns early in one's life of positive or negative thinking and behaving. These patterns reinforce self-confidence, whether low or high, and become habits. In some cases, these habits can be very destructive, causing us to feed and nurture feelings of low self-confidence even when there are no reasons for it. In other words, things in our lives may have changed significantly since childhood and we may no longer be subject to the influences and stored memory that contributed to our low self-confidence, yet we perpetuate it by our low self-belief and behaviors and negative thinking – we forget how to trust in ourselves and to be confident.

Arthur Ashe said, "One important key to success is self-confidence. An important key to self-confidence is preparation."

You can and must begin to believe in yourself to the point of knowing whatever you decide to do, perform, or complete will only be a matter of time to accomplish.

Here are some easy steps on how to be confident.

I. Appraising yourself and being able to raise your confidence is about liking yourself and appreciating your talents, abilities and attributes, such as problem solving and finding solutions to life's challenges. This does not mean becoming egotistical or vain. It merely means acknowledging your good traits and qualities. The self-concept – how you think about yourself – has a great deal to do with your confidence. If you continually tell yourself you are a failure, a loser, a poor student or whatever terms you use to put yourself down, you are feeding your lack of confidence and you will create a negative attitude. You are reinforcing what others wrongly caused you to feel about yourself. If you accept that they were wrong, or perhaps ignorant in doing this to you, why would you choose to do the same thing to yourself? It is time to be positive and build a more confident approach to life! It is time to believe, trust and have faith in yourself!

II. Basic solutions for bettering yourself and owning the key to success. Start and commit to a personal growth and self-improving regiment of determination. Being able to build good levels of confidence commands action; it is not an item you can wish for, buy or borrow. There are solutions you can engage in every single day when learning how to develop self-belief, faith, trust and how to be confident. You must daily be intentional about your confidence building. Your future success is hidden in your daily routine.

III. Begin a regiment of listening to recorded information of inspiration, motivation, those which have developed themselves to levels of success in areas of life. It is important to build a steady, consistent, program of listening and not stop. Repetition is critical to change your paradigm. Be steadfast in your endeavor to build your confidence. A 'coach' can be of an enormous benefit also.

Anthony Robbins says, "It's not what we do once in a while that shapes our lives. It's what we do consistently."

Jim Rohn says, "Success is neither magical nor mysterious. Success is the natural consequence of consistently applying basic fundamentals."

10)CHARACTER

Gifts and talents will get you there; Character will keep you there.

Character is defined as the mental and moral qualities distinctive to an individual. Merriam-Webster goes on to say this about character. The complex of mental and ethical traits marking and often individualizing a person, group, or nation.

I've place this 'C' at the very end of the book because just as discipline is to D7 Steps to Transforming, (which I travel the world teaching, training, and speaking on), so is character to the previous nine 'C's in this book. It is the foundational support for you to 'C' your way through. Character is the real you, it's the 'you' which shows up when things don't go right or not your way. It's the 'you' which responds to the difficult and trying times we face in a world which isn't always fair. It's the 'you' that appears when your back is against the wall and looks like all is lost. It's the 'you' when failure finds you and you're trying to decide is it worth it or should I go on. It's the 'you' when you need to make a choice or decision and no one's there but you. Character and integrity go hand in hand. The two are glued together. You cannot have a good character without integrity and you won't have integrity without a good character.

Integrity: Steadfast adherence to a strict moral or ethical code. When you combine character and integrity here' s what you get: character is one's moral and ethical code, and integrity means that one lives according to that code. Thus, someone who lives with integrity, lives according to their moral values.

In a published article research stated that when we are being watched, or perceive we are being watched, it has an impact on our social behavior and we tend to be on our best behavior when we feel that we are being observed. I believe it is a good practice to live each day with the I'm being watched mentality. Seeing that our character trait is our behavior when no one is looking then this brings about the fact that there is good and bad character in people. At least until we reach a level of behavior which is dictated by an honest, kind, and just life no matter what the situation may be.

Albert Einstein said, Weakness of attitude becomes weakness of character.

A good character is crucial in all of us but nowhere is it more necessary for those who find themselves in powerful and influential leadership positions. I was around when bad character leadership brought about the demise of such giant companies as Enron and WorldCom. Not to mention the countless others I could name. Not naming for derogatory reasons but for the need to realize character can build up or tear down. There come certain obligations with the privilege of leadership, one of which is that leaders need to instill trust in people that they will do the right things, regardless of whether they are being watched.

Brian Tracy says this about character. Your character is the degree to which you live your life consistent with high, life-enhancing values. A person who lacks character is one who compromises on higher order values in favor of lower order expedience, or who has no values at all. Your adherence to what you believe to be right and true is the real measure of the person you have become to this moment.

One of the facts of life is the difference between reputation and character. Reputation is the general opinion of others of a person whereas character is the distinctive qualities of an individual. Character takes years to build whereas reputation is built in a very short period. Character is who you are (internal), but reputation is how the society sees you (external). Some people are one way in public and totally different when they are home. Too many times we have heard of husbands who are one way in the community and abusers at home with their families. The best leaders lead through character guided by authenticity, while the one who leads from reputation are guided by image.

John Wooden said "Your reputation is who people think you are, your character is who you really are."

Character and reputation are two different words that people often interchange though there is a clear difference between them in meaning and connotation. Character can be defined as the distinctive qualities of an individual. Usually, when we refer to a person as one with a good character, it implies that the person has good qualities and lives by a sound moral and ethical code. This person may have good principles, to which he adheres in daily life. On the other hand, reputation refers to the general opinion held by others of an individual. The main difference between the two concepts is that while the character is more internal, reputation is rather external.

Helen Keller said, "Character cannot be developed in ease and quiet. Only through experience of trial and suffering can the soul be strengthened, ambition inspired, and success achieved".

Character is a vital attribute of a true leader and it is not a gift nor is the individual born with it. Character is developed, and it cannot be prayed for. No one can lay hands on a person and give them good character. Character is the ability to go through test and remain. Without character you have no foundation and when times are difficult you will sink as if in quick sand. So many people blow off the handle at the smallest incident because of lack of character. I am guilty of being the very same everywhere I go, at home, at the grocery store, at the bank, at meetings, and even in church. Recently I was told by someone who hadn't seen me in quite a while after we had spoken for some time that I was still the same person from years ago. Character means you don't have another life or another personality.

Character returns money when the clerk gives you back too much. My wife and I stopped at Sonic, a local burger establishment, and when the young person returns with the change it was more than I was supposed to receive. I use that opportunity to get the person to do some addition and subtraction in their mind. Once the error was realized I informed the young worker to keep all the change for a tip.

Are you a person of character? According to John Maxwell in Beyond Talent, "The choice to develop strong character may not be the most important to make the most of your talent. But it is certainly the most important to make sure you don't make the least of your talent." Character protects your talent – and allows you to build upon what you already have. To protect our talent, we must invest in that which is hidden below the surface. Like an iceberg, there is more than meets the eye. Strong character allows talent to hold up when storms come. John Maxwell, who happens to be my mentor, goes on to say, "Character creates a foundation upon which the structure of your talent and your life can build. If there are cracks in that foundation, you cannot build much."

John believes there are four core values which make up character. Self-discipline is the ability to do what is right even when you don't feel like doing it. Core values give order and structure to an individual's inner life, and when that inner life is in order, a person can navigate anything the world throws at him. John encourages us to write down our core values and strive to live them out each day. Those core values can be a guiding light during the darkest of moments. By following that "beacon," a leader has the chance to show that his or her talent is not just skin deep, but rather that it is protected and sustained by the heart. Next is a sense of identity. "No matter how hard you try, you cannot consistently behave in a way that is inconsistent to how you see yourself." Then there is integrity, which I addressed somewhat earlier. When values, thoughts, feelings, and actions are in alignment, a person becomes focused and his or her character is strengthened."

Bob Proctor says this about character. "There's no doubt that our character has a profound effect on our future. What we must remember, however, is not merely how powerful character is in influencing our destiny, but how powerful we are in shaping our own character and, therefore, our own destiny." Character may determine our fate, but character is not determined by fate. It's a common mistake to think of character as something that is fully formed and fixed very early in life. It calls to mind old maxims like "A leopard can't change its spots" and "You can't teach an old dog new tricks." This perspective that our character is "etched in stone" is supported by a great deal of modern psychology emphasizing self-acceptance. As Popeye says, "I am what I am." The hidden message is: Don't expect me to be more, better, or different.

Abraham Lincoln said, "Character is like a tree and reputation like a shadow. The shadow is what we think of it; the tree is the real thing."

Ultimately, these views of humanity totally undervalue the lifelong potential for growth that comes with the power of reflection and choice. How depressing it would be to believe that we can't choose to be better – more honest, more respectful, more responsible, and more caring. None of us should give up the personal quest to improve our character. Not because we're bad – we don't have to be sick to get better – but because we're not as good as we could be. There are so many things in life we can't control – whether we're beautiful or smart, whether we had good parents or bad, whether we grew up with affirmation or negation – it's uplifting to remember that nothing but moral will power is needed to make us better.

If possible, (and all things are when you believe), find you a life coach and allow him or her to assist you in your endeavor. Life coaching can be for personal or professional empowerment. Is life coaching for you? Most life coaches will offer a free introductory life coaching session.

You might be an executive or the owner of a successful small business looking to find balance between the demands of work and the needs of your family. You might be an empty-nester looking to make a difference in the lives of others but not sure which direction to choose. Maybe it's simply that you want your already great relationship to be spectacular.

Perhaps you are a musician, a writer, or an artist looking for a creative breakthrough, or a doctoral candidate looking for the perfect thesis. You might even be a twenty-something techno whiz entrepreneur with a brilliant idea for a product or service that will change the world forever. Maybe you just want to figure out how to have more fun. Whatever your circumstances, goals or dreams might be, the bottom line is that your life is in transition. Maybe you are determined to make your life be what you want it to be! That's where a professional life coach comes in and when professionally trained can help turn dreams into reality.

****** Here's what life coaching offers you: ******

As your life coach, we'll help you discover what's really most important to you in your life. Then we'll help you design a plan to achieve those things. We'll work with you to eliminate any obstacles or blocks that stand in your way. We'll partner with you all the way to success. Then we'll celebrate with you!

- About Us -

Calhoun & Calhoun, LLC umbrella several companies. Excellent Door Service aka Calhouns Garage Door Service, P & C Enterprises, In2Win Inc., the Winning Factor, our company which handles our speaking engagements, leadership training, and personal development. Mr. Calhoun is a John Maxwell Team Certified Coach, Speaker, Teacher, and Trainer. Senior Pastor of Full of Faith Christian Center Institute International. We've been assisting many to set, as well as, achieve life goals for over 25 years.

- Our Coaching Philosophy -

We believe that each of us has the wisdom and power within us to make our life be what we want it to be. We see the coaching relationship as an alliance, a partnership, a process of inquiry that empowers clients to reconnect with their own inner wisdom, to find their own answers, to rediscover those powerful moments of choice out of which lasting change grows.

We believe we are all whole beings with whole lives and that every choice we make affects every other aspect of our lives. Our work affects our relationships. Our relationships touch our spirituality. Our spiritual well-being affects our capacity for joy which affects our work and so on, round and round. We coach the whole person. We believe you deserve the life you want, so... Who are you? What is important to you? What are your challenges? What gets in your way? Where do you want to go? How would you feel if your life were just exactly the way you wanted it to be? When would you like to begin?

David Brinkley said, "A successful person is one who can lay a firm foundation with the bricks others have thrown at him."

Having two hands are so beneficial; One to help yourself, the second to help others.

Marianne Williamson said, "Nothing liberates our greatness like the desire to help, the desire to serve."

If you want to change the world, first change yourself, then tell others how you did it. Never demand that people change; Just inspire them to change using your own change as an example instead.

Visit us @

http://www.craycalhoun.com

Email: cray@motivatedwinners.com

Order these best-selling books:

YOU MUST 'C' YOUR WAY THROUGH

&

YOU CAN WIN IN LIFE!

T G B T G

ABOUT THE AUTHOR

From drug, alcohol addiction, bankruptcy, homelessness, and trouble with the law, C. Ray Calhoun rose to become a successful business owner, entrepreneur, certified coach, speaker, trainer, teacher with the John Maxwell Team, senior pastor, and a #1 best-selling author. He now speaks, trains, coach executives and individuals in personal growth, leadership, relationships, equipping, attitude, and cultural differences. He works with schools, businesses, and law enforcement agencies to improve their quality of leadership and community relations. Mr. Calhoun speaks to youth organizations, visits the jail and prisons, and encourages all to create the future they desire by daily choices. We desire to help YOU!

We recommend and offer material for you to read about life coaching

Take the Life Coaching Quiz

"Make Your Dreams Come True"

Contact us about life coaching & speaking

the Winning Factor, LLC

www.craycalhoun.com

www.motivatedwinners.com

Calhoun & Calhoun, LLC

- Privacy Policy -

Confidentiality is a sacred trust.

We never sell, rent, or trade our clients' personal data.

We never spam.

We accept online payments.

Fast - Free - Secure

Sign Up Now!

www.craycalhoun.com

All content on this site © 2016 the Winning Factor, LLC

Disclaimer: All content from the Winning Factor, LLC is provided for information and education purposes only. Individuals wishing to make changes to their dietary, lifestyle, exercise, or medication regimens should do so in conjunction with a competent, knowledgeable, medical and/or mental professional. Anyone who chooses to apply the information from the Winning Factor, LLC does so of their own volition and at their own risk. The owner of and contributors to the Winning Factor, LLC accept no responsibility or liability whatsoever for any harm - real or imagined - from the use or dissemination of information contained here. If these conditions are not agreeable to you, you are advised to pursue other resources immediately.

Copyright – 2016 tWF

www.ingramcontent.com/pod-product-compliance
Lightning Source LLC
Chambersburg PA
CBHW060054100426
42742CB00014B/2833